BPEL PM and OSB Operational Management with Oracle Enterprise Manager 10g Grid Control

Manage the operational tasks for multiple BPEL and OSB environments centrally

Narayan Bharadwaj

PACKT PUBLISHING

enterprise
professional expertise distilled

BIRMINGHAM - MUMBAI

BPEL PM and OSB Operational Management with Oracle Enterprise Manager 10*g* Grid Control

First published: August 2010

Production Reference: 2160810

Published by Packt Publishing Ltd.
32 Lincoln Road
Olton
Birmingham, B27 6PA, UK.

ISBN 978-1-847197-74-0

www.packtpub.com

Cover Image by Sandeep Babu (sandyjb@gmail.com)

Credits

Author
Narayan Bharadwaj

Reviewers
Hans Forbrich
Hector R. Madrid
Arvind Maheshwari
Matt Wright

Acquisition Editor
James Lumsden

Development Editor
Ved Prakash Jha

Technical Editor
Rukhsana Khambatta

Copy Editor
Sanchari Mukherjee

Editorial Team Leader
Gagandeep Singh

Project Team Leader
Priya Mukerjee

Project Coordinator
Ashwin Shetty

Proofreader
Sandra Hopper

Indexer
Rekha Nair

Production Coordinator
Adline Swetha Jesuthas

Cover Work
Adline Swetha Jesuthas

About the Author

Narayan Bharadwaj (aka Nadu) has dabbled in several different areas of the business software market. He has more than a decade of experience working in disparate technologies such as service-oriented architecture, systems management, and everything in between. Other technology areas include cloud computing, database, middleware, and IT management software. While dabbling in these technologies, Narayan wore several hats—from software consultant, database administrator, application developer, to product manager. Prior to these gigs, he went to school at the University of Maryland, and the Indian Institute of Technology, Kharagpur, to pursue various technical degrees. Thinking this was not good enough, he added an MBA from the Haas School of Business at the University of California, Berkeley.

Narayan spent close to a decade at Oracle USA Inc at Redwood Shores, CA, where he was the group product manager for management of middleware and service-oriented architecture products. During his stint at the Application and Systems Management Products division, Narayan led the charge into new markets such as real-user monitoring, Java application diagnostics, middleware management, and service-oriented architecture management. This included key acquisitions such as Moniforce, ClearApp, and AmberPoint. More recently, Narayan has moved to the clouds in San Francisco, leading Salesforce.com's platform strategy and execution with respect to cloud management and cloud data analytics. He lives in San Mateo, CA, with his wife and two-year-old son.

When he is not commuting to work, pursuing degrees, or wearing different hats, Narayan loves to wield a racket on a badminton or tennis court, spike a volley ball, or run the half marathon once in a long while.

> I am constantly inspired by the two women in my life—my mother and my wife. Thank you for being there for me.

About the Reviewers

Hans Forbrich is a well-known member of the Oracle Community. He started with Oracle products in 1984 and has kept abreast of nearly all of Oracle's Core Technologies. As ACE Director, Hans has been invited to present at Oracle Open World and various Oracle User Group meetings around the world. His company, Forbrich Computer Consulting Ltd., is well established in western Canada. Hans specializes in delivering Oracle University training through Oracle University and partners such as Exit Certified.

Although his special interests include Oracle Spatial, OracleVM, and Oracle Enterprise Linux, Hans has been particularly excited about the advances in Oracle SOA, Oracle WebLogic, and Oracle Grid Control.

Hans has been a technical reviewer for a number of Packt Publishing books, including *"Mastering Oracle Scheduler in Oracle 11g Databases," "Oracle 10g/11g Data and Database Management Utilities,"* and *"Oracle VM Manager 2.1.2."*

I wish to thank my wife Susanne, and the Edmonton Opera, for their patience while I work on these reviews as well as on my own book.

Hector R. Madrid is the author of the *"Oracle 10g/11g Data and Database Management Utilities"* book. He is currently working as a freelance consultant; he collaborates with Oracle University as a certified instructor for the DBA, Java, and Application Server course tracks. He is a highly respected Oracle professional with 20 years of experience as a full-time DBA. He works with a wide range of DBA requirements starting with the daily DBA duties to the tasks related to mission-critical and high-availability systems. He was the first Oracle Certified Master in Latin America. He obtained a Master's Degree in Computer Sciences from the Metropolitan Autonomous University (UAM) and he has presented different technical papers at several Oracle conferences.

I want to thank my family for their patience and the time I borrowed from them during the revision of this book.

Arvind Maheshwari, a senior Software Development Manager for the Oracle Enterprise Manager development team, is focused on building management solutions for middleware. He has more than 15 years of experience in the IT industry and has played the role of developer, consultant, architect, and technical manager in the financial, manufacturing, and telecom industries, developing enterprise solutions that are deployed in high-availability architectures.

Matt Wright is a director at Rubicon Red, an independent consulting firm helping customers enable enterprise agility and operational excellence through the adoption of emerging technologies such as Service-Oriented Architecture (SOA), Business Process Management (BPM), and Cloud Computing.

With over 20 years of experience in building enterprise-scale distributed systems, Matt first became involved with SOA shortly after the initial submission of SOAP 1.1 to the W3C in 2000, and has worked with some of the early adopters of BPEL since its initial release in 2002. Since then, he has been engaged in some of the earliest SOA-based implementations across EMEA and APAC.

Prior to Rubicon Red, Matt held various senior roles within Oracle, most recently as Director of Product Management for Oracle Fusion Middleware in APAC, where he was responsible for working with organizations to educate and enable them in realizing the full business benefits of SOA in solving complex business problems.

As a recognized authority on SOA, Matt is a regular speaker and instructor at private and public events. He also enjoys writing and publishes his own blog (`http://blog.rubiconred.com`). Matt holds a B.Sc. (Eng) in Computer Science from Imperial College, University of London.

Table of Contents

Preface

Oracle Enterprise Manager has been around for more than a decade, and many database administrators around the world have used one or more Enterprise Manager products for running their databases more efficiently. Over the past few years, Enterprise Managers have made a big push to manage middleware and applications as well. This has helped change the original market perception that Enterprise Manager was simply a DBA's best friend.

With its flagship Grid Control product release 10.2.0.5 (released on Linux platforms in February 2009), Enterprise Manager has strengthened its previous offerings in the middleware area. Enterprise Manager's strategic direction is consistent with the one charted out by Oracle after completing the BEA acquisition on April 29, 2008. The greatest improvements have been made in managing WebLogic Server, and the Oracle SOA platform that includes Oracle BPEL Process Manager, and Oracle Service Bus (formerly AquaLogic Service Bus).

Enterprise Manager has made several acquisitions in the past two years to complement existing capabilities and provide a complete management solution to users. Auptyma was the first of these acquisitions, which provided deep Java diagnostic capabilities without instrumentation or overhead in production environments. The product was renamed to Application Diagnostics for Java (AD4J). Separately, Moniforce was acquired to manage an end user's experience while interacting with an application and service providers, and the product was renamed to Real User Experience Insight (RUEI). Another key acquisition was ClearApp—a company that provided technology to model and monitor composite applications. The product was renamed to Composite Application Modeler and Monitor (CAMM).

Several integration challenges lie ahead, and many still think of Enterprise Manager as a database management solution. The product has grown considerably faster in the past two years, especially in the middleware, SOA, and application space. Enterprise Manager is one of the top product lines at Oracle, but is still the best kept secret in the Oracle portfolio. With a vast array of product lines, it is important for an Oracle customer's IT to manage these product lines centrally, and with a low cost of ownership. The big four management vendors (CA, IBM, HP, BMC) have broad product offerings that are not optimized for Oracle products. Further, the pure play vendors are focused on niche areas, and do not provide an enterprise management solution. Oracle Enterprise Manager plays an important role for enterprises that have one or more Oracle products in their data center, as well as non-Oracle products.

Who this book is for

If you are involved with Oracle BPEL Process Manager, Oracle SOA Suite, or Oracle Service Bus, then you are the right candidate for this book. You are an even better candidate if you support the operational infrastructure for any of these products. For a long time, application and SOA administrators have longed for visibility into the distributed service-based environment. If you or your team supports any of these products in a production environment, you will know the pain of dealing with day-to-day operational issues. This book will go a long way to alleviate some of those problems using Enterprise Manager capabilities.

If you are an SOA architect or associated with SOA governance in any way (for example, an SOA Center of Excellence), this book will serve as an eye opener to the many features available to gain production assurance in complex SOA environments. This will help you govern the SOA environment in conjunction with other tools such as Oracle Enterprise Repository (OER), Oracle Service Registry (OSR), and Oracle Web Services Manager (OWSM). However, this book shall focus on runtime SOA management with Enterprise Manager Grid Control.

If you like a functional approach to solving your operational problems, this is the right book for you. You will find that the book avoids lecturing on concepts, and takes a direct approach to solving real operational problems.

A general awareness of service-oriented architecture is expected, as well as an awareness of the Oracle SOA products such as BPEL Process Manager and Oracle Service Bus. No specific management or operational expertise is required. This book will help set up the framework for managing the Oracle SOA products using a step-by-step functional-based approach.

What you should find in the book

This book contains details on how to set up and automate various operational tasks essential for the smooth running of Oracle SOA products in production. It will walkthrough step-by-step exercises to assist the administrator in managing these products from a single web-based console. It will relieve the administrator from performing mundane time-consuming repetitive tasks.

What you won't find

The book avoids going through explanations on SOA, BPEL, or Service Bus. This is not the right book if you want to develop BPEL and OSB services from tools such as JDeveloper. Also, it avoids talking about basic Grid Control product issues such as download and installation, other than the first chapter.

What this book covers

The introductory chapter contains basic information that is a prerequisite for the other chapters. You can dive into the other chapters on a need basis, based on what you would like to accomplish. All chapters have a problem statement defined, along with a summary of the solution provided. The solution itself is a step-by-step walkthrough on how to accomplish certain tasks to solve the problem.

The book is divided into three sections. The first section covers the management of BPEL Process Manager with Grid Control. The second section focuses on management of SOA Suite in general. The third section covers management of Oracle Service Bus.

Chapter 1, Grid Control, BPEL, and OSB Overview, gives a basic introduction to Grid Control that includes download, installation, and basic configuration. This is the foundation technology that provides the infrastructure for managing various targets from a single console.

I: BPEL Management

Chapter 2, Discovering BPEL PM, talks about the discovery and configuration of the BPEL Process Manager target. Discovery of BPEL PM as a Grid Control-managed target is the first step before performing other management tasks.

Chapter 3, BPEL Process Monitoring, talks about viewing deployed BPEL processes and their constituent partner links. It goes on to talk about monitoring of BPEL processes and partner links using a combination of metrics and synthetic tests.

Chapter 4, BPEL Infrastructure Management, describes how to manage the underlying infrastructure components such as BPEL Process Manager server, dehydration database, Application Server, host, and so on. Administrators can manage several disparate systems in groups, reducing the time to detect the root cause of system-related problems.

Chapter 5, BPEL Service-Level Management, describes how to set service-level expectations for BPEL Processes, partner links, and tracking those levels through various metrics. This enables the service providers to monitor agreed-upon contractual guarantees with service consumers.

Chapter 6, BPEL Services Dashboard, illustrates that dashboards are important to visualize service-level performance and metrics for key services. This chapter also walks through how to construct a simple dashboard to show all critical services, and their top metrics, including service levels. Operations typically use this to keep a ready eye on services and act on any deviations from expected SLAs.

Chapter 7, BPEL Deployment Automation, shows deployment of BPEL artifacts is a repetitive and time-consuming task. This chapter describes how to deploy BPEL artifacts to multiple servers in an automated fashion. This ensures deployments are conducted in an error-free manner, and reduces overall scheduled downtime.

Chapter 8, BPEL Configuration Management, describes how to manage the configuration settings of the BPEL infrastructure, including setting baselines, and comparisons. This helps to diagnose problems due to configuration changes as well as standardize configurations across the enterprise.

II: SOA Suite Management

Chapter 9, SOA Suite Cloning, discusses cloning as a complex administrative task that needs deep product expertise. This chapter walks through a simple scenario to clone an existing SOA Suite from one instance to another. Administrators can use this to perform critical time-consuming tasks in a standardized, error-free manner.

Chapter 10, Web Application Monitoring, describes how to set and monitor Web services using Grid Control service models, SLA rules, and synthetic tests. Web applications can also be monitored — including the recording and playback of HTTP(s) transactions to troubleshoot problems. Application administrators can proactively monitor applications from an end-user perspective.

III: WebLogic and Oracle Service Bus Management

Chapter 11, Discovery of WebLogic and OSB targets, talks about managing multiple WebLogic domains and OSB instances from a single console, as it is a frequent problem for the middleware administrator. Middleware administrators can use a single console to manage all their installations, perform complex management tasks, and dive into their respective WebLogic or OSB console to perform administrative activities. All of this enables the administrator to standardize management tasks, and hence the behavior of WebLogic and OSB servers, leading to increased uptime.

Chapter 12, OSB Deployment Automation, discusses that deployment of OSB projects and resources to multiple domains can be cumbersome and time consuming. This chapter walks through typical deployment scenarios and how they can be automated using the deployment procedure framework. This enables infrastructure teams to standardize deployments, as well as to track and manage artifacts centrally.

Chapter 13, OSB Proxy and Business Service Monitoring, walks the reader through Oracle Service Bus services that provide a versatile frontend plumbing layer to standardize messages from various sources and differing formats. Any performance bottleneck directly relates to a slowdown in critical backend business processes. This chapter also covers the monitoring capabilities for OSB proxy and business services. These provide the administrator with visibility into the runtime behavior, and take proactive steps to maintain a high-performing environment.

Chapter 14, WebLogic and OSB Configuration Management, describes that configuration changes are a major cause of downtimes in production environments. This chapter also covers WebLogic and OSB configuration tracking, viewing changes, and comparing and saving configurations. This enables administrators to resolve problems quickly and standardize a set of configurations across the enterprise.

What you need for this book

The target product versions used throughout this book are installed on Oracle Enterprise Linux platform and share an Oracle database 10.2.0.2 as the common repository. For the first two sections, Oracle SOA Suite is used as the target. SOA Suite 10.1.3.x is installed in a single node environment on Oracle Application Server 10.1.3.x. The popular SOA Order Booking application is used throughout the book to illustrate various features. Oracle Service Bus 10*g*R3 installed on WebLogic Server 10*g*R3 is used as the target for the third section. The Mortgage Broker application is used to illustrate various features.

Enterprise Manager Grid Control 10gR5 or 10.2.0.5 is used in all the exercises. It is installed with a single Oracle Managed Server (OMS) and two agents—one for the SOA Suite and another one for Oracle Service Bus.

Conventions

In this book, you will find a number of styles of text that distinguish between different kinds of information. Here are some examples of these styles, and an explanation of their meaning.

Code words in text are shown as follows: "Select `bpel_parallel_flow.jar` for the current example."

New terms and **important words** are shown in bold. Words that you see on the screen, in menus or dialog boxes for example, appear in our text like this: "From the BPEL target home page, click on the **Processes** tab".

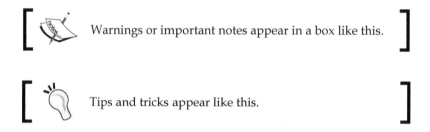

Warnings or important notes appear in a box like this.

Tips and tricks appear like this.

Reader feedback

Feedback from our readers is always welcome. Let us know what you think about this book—what you liked or may have disliked. Reader feedback is important for us to develop titles that you really get the most out of.

To send us general feedback, simply drop an email to `feedback@packtpub.com`, and mention the book title in the subject of your message.

If there is a book that you need and would like to see us publish, please send us a note in the **SUGGEST A TITLE** form on `www.packtpub.com` or email `suggest@packtpub.com`.

If there is a topic that you have expertise in and you are interested in either writing or contributing to a book, see our author guide on `www.packtpub.com/authors`.

Customer support

Now that you are the proud owner of a Packt book, we have a number of things to help you to get the most from your purchase.

Errata

Although we have taken every care to ensure the accuracy of our contents, mistakes do happen. If you find a mistake in one of our books—maybe a mistake in text or code—we would be grateful if you would report this to us. By doing so, you can save other readers from frustration, and help us to improve subsequent versions of this book. If you find any errata, please report them by visiting http://www.packtpub.com/support, selecting your book, clicking on the **errata submission form** link, and entering the details of your errata. Once your errata are verified, your submission will be accepted and the errata added to any list of existing errata. Any existing errata can be viewed by selecting your title from http://www.packtpub.com/support.

Piracy

Piracy of copyright material on the Internet is an ongoing problem across all media. At Packt, we take the protection of our copyright and licenses very seriously. If you come across any illegal copies of our works in any form on the Internet, please provide us with the location address or website name immediately so that we can pursue a remedy.

Please contact us at copyright@packtpub.com with a link to the suspected pirated material.

We appreciate your help in protecting our authors, and our ability to bring you valuable content.

Questions

You can contact us at questions@packtpub.com if you are having a problem with any aspect of the book, and we will do our best to address it.

1
Grid Control, BPEL, and OSB Overview

Management of hardware, software, and application components is important. In bad economic times, it is critical to get the maximum return from software and hardware investments, and for that an enterprise needs a sound management strategy. A management solution not only helps increase returns on existing investments, but also controls the cost of owning these investments. Enterprises today cannot be successful without such a solution.

In the SOA world, management is even more critical, as it governs distributed services and service infrastructures. The value from SOA investments cannot be realized without a sound management strategy. Operational management is becoming the centerpiece of the SOA Governance framework in most enterprises. Unless there is visibility and control on production environments, SOA project costs will exceed the accrued benefits. Management cannot be a bolt on after the implementation; it has to be a strategic part of the overall solution. It is beneficial to start thinking about the management strategy upfront, and implement it in conjunction with the SOA integrations. Further, all aspects of management need to be analyzed, and the right ones need to be implemented for the SOA integrations in the enterprise. Some of the key management areas are infrastructure monitoring, synthetic monitoring, configuration management, deployment automation, and business process execution monitoring. All of these need to be considered for the success of SOA projects.

In this chapter, we will provide a brief overview of the following products that will be covered throughout this book:

- Grid Control
  - ○ Overview
  - ○ Architecture and deployment
  - ○ Download and install
  - ○ Home page

- Oracle BPEL Process Manager overview
- Oracle SOA Suite overview
- Oracle Service Bus overview

Grid Control

Enterprise Manager Grid Control provides a single interface for managing thousands of disparate targets such as operating systems, databases, application servers, and packaged applications. It determines overall target health, tracks target inventory, automates target deployments, and manages service levels. All the historic monitoring information is stored in a database, and aggregated over time. This is complemented with a reporting and dashboard framework, which provides a summary to administrators as well as IT managers. Grid Control supports monitoring and management of a wide variety of hardware, software, and applications, and is really the tool of choice for Oracle products. It has capabilities for monitoring third-party products as well, either natively, or through plugins and connectors. The Grid Control framework can be extended using either plugins or connectors. This is made possible by a software development kit that comes out of the box with Grid Control. A good example of a plugin is if you want to monitor a specific hardware component that is not supported by Grid Control, you can extend the framework and add logic to monitor your specific hardware component. A connector, on the other hand, can be used to integrate Grid Control with other systems such as incident management systems (for example, Remedy Helpdesk or Oracle Business Activity Monitoring (Oracle BAM)).

Most chapters in this book cut across multiple versions of Grid Control. Concepts such as service-level management, infrastructure management, service-level dashboards, web application management, and configuration management are uniform across multiple Grid Control versions. That being said, this book will focus on Grid Control version 10.2.0.5, also referred to as 10gR5. This version was released on Linux platforms in February 2009, ported to other platforms during the rest of the year. Most of the chapters are valid for the prior version of Grid Control 10.2.0.4 (or 10gR4) as well. The notable exception is the third section that deals with managing the Oracle Service Bus. Enterprise Manager functionality for managing BPEL Process Manager is part of Grid Control 10.2.0.3 and above. The Oracle Service Bus management functionality was introduced with Grid Control 10.2.0.5.

Architecture and deployment

Grid Control has a three-tier architecture. The main components are the **Oracle Management Server** (**OMS**), the Management Agents (Agent), and the **Oracle Management Repository** (**OMR**). The central web-based console is available through popular browsers. The components are detailed as follows:

- **Oracle Management Server (OMS)**: This is the central engine, which accumulates information from all the distributed Management Agents. It provides the data for the web-based console, and persists the data in the Management Repository. Further, the OMS also executes the alerting rule logic, and the notification logic, as well as sending instructions to the agent for management tasks such as deployment.

- **Management Agent**: The agent is a lightweight C-program running on a server or host. This program typically collects all the monitoring and configuration information for the host, and the other targets on that host such as database, application server, SOA suite, and so on. The agent is also suitable for running operations at the host level through scripts. This capability is useful for taking corrective action (when a threshold is violated), or performing complex patching, or other deployment tasks. There is also the option of having remote agents, the only drawback being that the host metrics will not be collected.

- **Oracle Management Repository (OMR)**: The repository is a preconfigured Oracle database that comes packaged with Grid Control. No separate license is needed for the OMR. The OMS contains current and historical monitoring and configuration information from various agents. It comes with prebuilt schemas and PL/SQL procedures and functions to aggregate the data over different time periods.

- **Central web console**: The web console provides a window to all the rich information in the OMR. Each target type (for example, application server) has a home page with monitoring, alerting, configuration, and other specific information. The home page displays summary information across multiple targets. Reports and dashboards can be used to create custom views.

This book avoids going into deep discussions on deployments that are already addressed by product documentation or white papers. A basic knowledge of installing and configuring the Grid Control components are assumed. More information on architecture and deployment best practices is available on the Enterprise Manager pages on the **Oracle Technology Network (OTN)** at: http://www.oracle.com/technology/products/oem/ent_mgr/arch_dep.html

The following simple architecture diagram shows the main Grid Control components and their relationships:

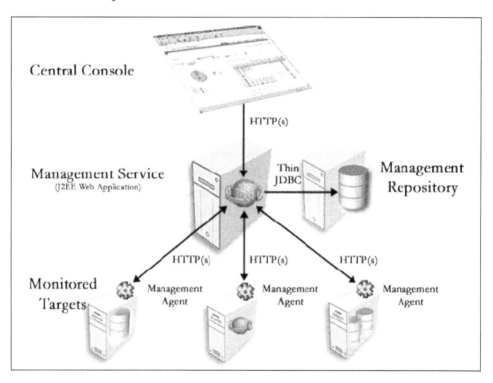

Installing Grid Control

The latest version of Grid Control can be downloaded from OTN at:
`http://www.oracle.com/technology/software/products/oem/index.html`

Grid Control documentation including installation, configuration, deployment modes, and so on can be found at: `http://download.oracle.com/docs/cd/B16240_01/doc/nav/portal_booklist.htm`

Once Grid Control is installed and configured, the SOA-related targets can be added. The prerequisite is to install a Management Agent (Agent) to the server that hosts the SOA Suite. More details on getting started with Grid Control SOA Management is available at the Oracle Technology Network (OTN) website: `http://download.oracle.com/docs/cd/B16240_01/doc/em.102/e12650/toc.htm`

Home page

After downloading and installing Grid Control, the first task is to view the home page of Grid Control. To view Grid Control home page on your local browser:

1. Navigate to `http://<your_server_name>:<server_port>/ememememem`.

2. Login as `sysman.sysman`. Use the password you set during the installation.

Following is the Enterprise Manager 10*g* Grid Control entry point or home page. The home page rolls up all the important information (starting in the upper-left corner):

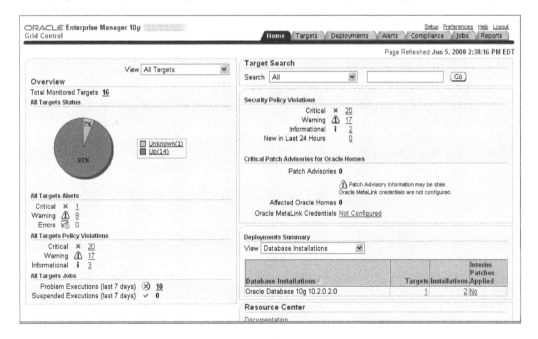

- **All Targets Status**: This section shows the total number of monitored Oracle targets. The pie chart shows their overall SLA availability and corresponding open alerts. This summary page can be rolled up for any target type.

  Click on the **View** dropdown and observe the different target types in this enterprise. This is a subset of the target types supported by Grid Control.

- **All Target Alerts**: Violations of thresholds for all metrics for the monitored targets, separated into **Critical** and **Warning** categories. **Errors** are Agent-related problems (Agent unreachable, cannot upload, metric collection error, and so on).

- **All Targets Policy Violations**: Over 300 Oracle best practices (for example, open port on Application Server) are coded in as policies in Grid Control. The Agent checks these policies daily and flag the violations.

- **Target Search**: Quickly access any target by simply typing in part of the target name.

- **Critical Patch Advisories for Oracle Homes**: Push any security alerts that are vital to your systems. Set up a connection to meta link and automatically download patch information for monitored Oracle homes.

- **Deployments Summary**: Enterprise Manager collects information on your entire configuration including software, patches (OS and Oracle software level), hardware, and so on. This is a rollup of all of the hosts, software, and OS(s) in your enterprise.

Oracle BPEL Process Manager overview

*Business Process Execution Language (BPEL), short for **Web Services Business Process Execution Language** (**WS-BPEL**) is an executable language for specifying interactions with Web Services. Processes in Business Process Execution Language export and import information by using Web Service interfaces exclusively. Source:* http://en.wikipedia.org/wiki/Business_Process_Execution_Language

Major vendors such as Oracle, Microsoft, and IBM are onboard with the BPEL standard, which has become the orchestration standard of choice. Oracle acquired a small company called Collaxa in 2005, which had an implementation of the BPEL standard, then renamed the product to BPEL Process Manager and made it the foundation of the SOA Suite. This also became the strategic technology product under the Fusion Middleware umbrella, as well as the Fusion Applications umbrella. Oracle Applications Unlimited (E-Business Suite, PeopleSoft, Siebel, Retek, and so on) use several different workflow technologies such as Oracle Workflow, but the roadmap for all these workflow technologies is to converge into the common BPEL standard, based on the Oracle BPEL Process Manager product. In short, this technology has huge implications not only for the overall middleware market, but also for the packaged applications market. Oracle, with its huge installed base in both the markets, especially after the acquisition of BEA in 2008, is focused on expanding the already large adoption of BPEL within its customer base.

BPEL Process Manager 10.1.2 was the first release after the Collaxa acquisition. Currently, the product is available as part of the Oracle SOA Suite 10.1.3.x. This is a fairly mature release of product, and has enjoyed widespread adoption among customers interested in implementing an SOA strategy. This is also the foundation of the next generation Oracle Fusion Applications.

Oracle SOA Suite overview

Oracle SOA Suite 10.1.3.x consists of three components—Oracle BPEL Process Manager, **Oracle Enterprise Service Bus** (OESB), and **Oracle Web Services Manager** (OWSM). Additionally, it also includes **Oracle Service Bus** (OSB), **Oracle Business Activity Monitoring (BAM)**, and the Rules Engine.

Oracle built an Enterprise Service Bus (OESB) as the plumbing layer to frontend the BPEL-based business processes. The Service Bus is used as the mediator layer to transform messages in different formats to common canonical formats, and route to the backend BPEL processes, or other services. It is a step up from the point-to-point **Enterprise Application Integration (EAI)** methodology that involves frequent changes at both ends of the integration.

Oracle SOA Suite 10.1.3.x is a single installable, and is extremely easy to install and configure with Oracle JDeveloper. As the common IDE to develop BPEL-based business processes, and OESB-based services it provides a great platform for developers and architects to implement SOA projects.

Oracle Service Bus overview

Oracle Service Bus is a proven, lightweight and scalable SOA integration platform that delivers low-cost, standards-based integration for high-volume, mission critical SOA environments. It is designed to connect, mediate, and manage interactions between heterogeneous services, legacy applications, packaged applications and multiple enterprise service bus (ESB) instances across an enterprise-wide service network. Oracle Service Bus is a core component in the Oracle SOA Suite as a backbone for SOA messaging. Source: `http://www.oracle.com/technologies/soa/service-bus.html`

With the acquisition of BEA, the **AquaLogic Service Bus (ALSB)** joined the Oracle family as well. ALSB was renamed to Oracle Service Bus (OSB) post acquisition. On July 1, 2008, Thomas Kurian, the Senior Vice President of Fusion Middleware, announced the strategic roadmap for Oracle middleware and BEA products. He announced that OSB would be the strategic service bus going forward, with its wide customer adoption, and advanced product capabilities.

Summary

With a single management solution to manage SOA services and infrastructure, and products, Grid Control reduces the complexity of an SOA environment. Grid Control is an enterprise-wide solution, so care must be taken to make it into a strategic product. The installation and deployment is not a trivial task. However, it is imperative to set up the management framework to meet the needs of the enterprise.

Grid Control has traditionally been viewed as a database management solution, but this book will highlight the necessity of using this solution for SOA environments.

In this chapter, we looked at some fundamental concepts of the target products, as well as the management solution. In particular, we discussed Enterprise Manager Grid Control as an important management solution. Briefly, we discussed the installation, documentation, and architecture of Grid Control. Then we discussed the SOA products BPEL PM and OSB. We introduced the basic concepts for both products, and a brief background for each.

This was simply an overview of these products. A good administrator should have basic working knowledge of Oracle BPEL PM, SOA Suite, and Service Bus. This book will focus on the next step, which is to manage these products from Grid Control.

The next few chapters will walkthrough hands-on exercises to set up and perform management tasks.

2
Discovering BPEL PM

A management solution needs to locate and identify whatever it needs to manage. This process is called discovery, where the management solution locates and identifies all the targets. This is typically done using management agents that are deployed on servers that contain the targets that need to be managed. Discovery of targets enables administrators to have a picture of the environment along with the various components that need to be managed.

For any small, medium, or large enterprise, the challenge is to manage several disparate targets from a single console. The traditional hardware and software components such as servers, storage devices, operating systems, databases, middleware, and applications have been managed by system management solutions. However, a new breed of BPEL-based applications and infrastructure poses new problems. First, they need to be managed along with existing hardware and software. Second, as the BPEL projects proliferate across the enterprise, the infrastructure team is faced with increasing problems to manage these projects. Third, for the administrators who are new to BPEL, supporting these environments in production poses unknown challenges. Finally, the IT managers want to avoid hiring new administrators with increasing BPEL projects.

Grid Control provides a way to discover the BPEL components, whether it's on production or otherwise. For the infrastructure team, this is a convenient way to manage several installations from one console. Once the agent is installed on each of the servers hosting BPEL PM, the discovery process can be initiated from the console.

In this chapter, we will discuss how to discover and configure a BPEL Process Manager target. Discovery of BPEL PM targets is the first step before performing other management tasks. Further, creating the infrastructure service is mandatory to manage BPEL processes and related infrastructure. The following areas are covered in this chapter:

- Support for managing BPEL PM
- BPEL PM target discovery
    - Navigating to application servers
    - Discovering a BPEL PM target
    - Navigating to the BPEL PM target home page
    - Configuring a BPEL PM target

Support for managing BPEL PM

The BPEL PM product ships with a console that is useful for administration activities such as turning a process on or off, deleting instances, checking the flow of an instance, and so on. However, it cannot provide management capabilities such as monitoring the availability and health of the servers, processes, configuration management, and bulk deployment.

Grid Control introduced BPEL management functionality with the 10.2.0.3 (or 10*g*R3) version, released in January 2007. The first release provided most of the functionality for monitoring the BPEL infrastructure including the BPEL PM server. Additionally, it had process-level monitoring, error-instance management, and service-level management.

The 10.2.0.4 (10*g*R4) version, released on Linux platforms in November 2007, brought additional new features for managing BPEL PM. Configuration management, deployment automation, and adapter monitoring were the main features of the release. The 10.2.0.5 (10*g*R5) version, released on Linux platforms in February 2009, added reporting capabilities for tracking troublesome BPEL instances.

BPEL PM target discovery

This set of step-by-step exercises will walkthrough the discovery of a BPEL PM target and setting up monitoring configuration for the target.

Navigating to application servers

As the SOA Suite and BPEL Process Manager server is hosted on an application server (for example, Oracle Application Server, Oracle WebLogic Server), the first task is to visit the application server home page:

1. Navigate to `http://<Grid_Control_server_name>:<server_port>/em`.

2. Log in as *sysman*. Use the password you set during the installation.

3. Click on the **Targets** tab.

4. Click on the **Middleware** sub-tab.

> This is a view showing all of the monitored application servers (Oracle AS, BEA WebLogic, and so on) within the enterprise. For each target, a summary of status with details, alerts, policy violations, CPU usage, and memory usage on the host are tabulated.

Discovering a BPEL PM target

The administrator needs to inform Grid Control to explicitly discover the application server and the associated targets such as BPEL PM. Before attempting discovery, the Grid Control Agent (10.2.0.3 or higher) needs to be installed on the host with the application server software. Note that a remote agent can also be used to discover an application server. The only drawback with a remote agent is the host and operating system metrics for the application server machine will not be picked up.

1. As shown in the following screenshot, from the drop-down list on the right, add an **Oracle Application Server** target. Click on **Go**.

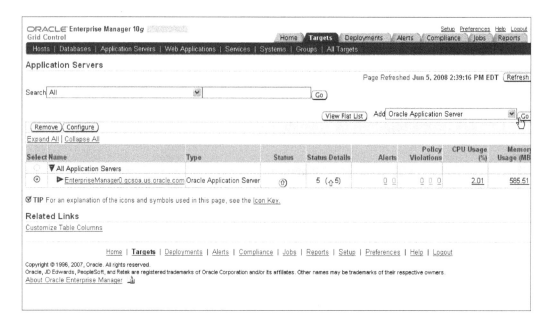

2. On the **Add Application Server** page:
    ° Click on the *flashlight* icon to pick a host.
    ° In the pop-up window, select the radio button for the host and click on **Select**, as shown in the following screenshot:

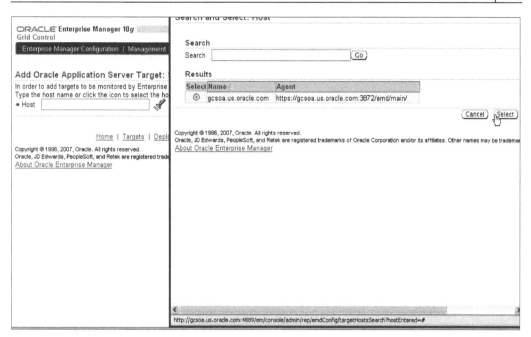

3. On the **Add Application Server** page, click on **Continue** on the right.

4. On the **Discover Application Server: Results** page, click on **OK.**

5. In a very short time, you should get a confirmation page. Click on **OK.**

6. On the **Application Servers** page, click on **Expand All** and view your application server.

Notice the components of this application server. Notice the two **OC4J** targets, as well as the **Oracle BPEL Process Manager** target.

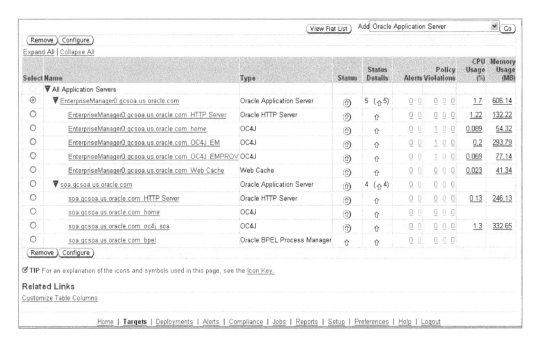

Navigating to the BPEL PM target home page

The BPEL PM target is a child target of the application server target. There are multiple ways to navigate to the home page of the BPEL PM target; the most common path is to click on the Oracle BPEL Process Manager target name hyperlink.

 On the Oracle BPEL Process Manager home pages, you will see the **Status** label, which shows the availability status of the BPEL PM server, **Availability** (%) (last 24 hours), **Oracle Home**, and **Host**.

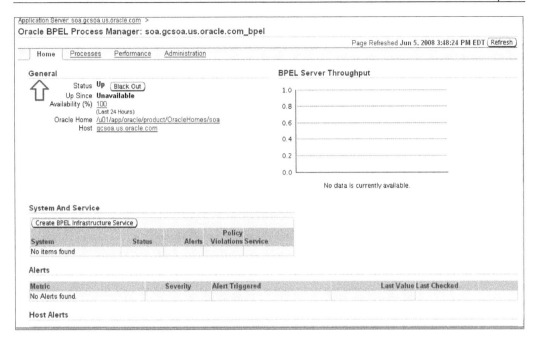

Configuring a BPEL PM target

Once the BPEL PM target is discovered, the administrator needs to provide the target with basic configuration information. This enables the BPEL target in Grid Control to talk to the BPEL PM server. This communication is needed because the BPEL target collects out-of-box monitoring metric data by polling the BPEL PM server through APIs.

1. Under the **Related Links** section at the bottom, click on **Monitoring Configuration**.

2. Enter the administrator username for BPEL Process Manager as **oc4jadmin**.

3. Enter the password for the administrator as *welcome1*.

4. Enter the **Initial Context Factory** as **com.evermind.server.rmi. RMIInitialContextFactory**.

5. Enter the **Context Provider URL** as

   opmn:ormi://<Application_Server_Host_Name>:6003:oc4j_soa/orabpel.

6. Leave the other fields blank and click on **OK**, as shown in the following screenshot:

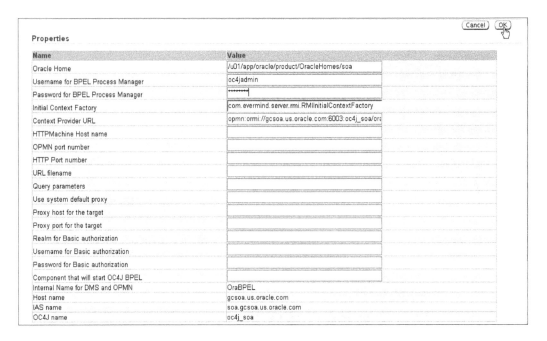

This concludes the discovery and configuration of the BPEL PM target deployed on Oracle Application Server.

Summary

Discovery is the first step to manage a target in the enterprise. Discovering and managing multiple targets from a single console is a powerful way to ramp up on new projects while maintaining a standardized management platform. This avoids hiring new administrators for new projects that increase the number of managed targets.

In this chapter, we looked at how to discover and configure the BPEL PM target.

These are mandatory steps to enable subsequent management tasks. We discovered the BPEL PM target indirectly by discovering the application server (in this case Oracle Application Server). Note that the discovery process is similar for discovering BPEL PM targets installed on WebLogic and WebSphere application servers. Detailed discovery information (including 10.2.0.4 patches) for WebLogic and WebSphere application server-based BPEL PM is listed in the following document on Oracle Technology Network:

`http://download.oracle.com/docs/cd/B16240_01/doc/em.102/e12650/toc.htm`.

The next few chapters will walkthrough hands-on exercises to set up and perform additional management tasks for the discovered BPEL PM target.

3
BPEL Process Monitoring

It is important to understand the complexity of a BPEL process that creates the additional need for active operational monitoring. BPEL processes are the new generation of workflow. They are SOA enabled, which means they orchestrate interactions between different systems using a common **Web Service Invocation Framework (WSIF)**. WSIF enables BPEL to build a façade to interact with any system that is Web service enabled. The Web service interactions are called "partner links" in the BPEL framework. This is quite powerful for orchestrating complex business processes that involve new and legacy systems. It provides IT with an automated framework for enterprise-wide business processes. Monitoring BPEL processes is important for business analysts and administrators to maintain business visibility and resolve problems quickly. This chapter talks about viewing deployed BPEL processes and their constituent partner links. Further, monitoring of BPEL processes and partner links using a combination of metrics and synthetic tests is covered.

Grid Control provides means to monitor critical BPEL processes, partner links, and Web services through service tests to determine availability and response time. Grid Control also provides a means of measuring critical metrics for actual requests initiated against each of the Web services deployed on the container. With a combined end-user and request perspective, Grid Control can determine the service availability of all monitored services.

- Challenges
- Solution
- Step-by-step exercises:
    - ° Navigating to the BPEL PM target home page
    - ° Navigating to the BPEL process home page
    - ° Creating the BPEL process aggregate service
    - ° Creating a SOAP test to monitor a partner link
    - ° Creating a SOAP test to monitor a BPEL process
    - ° Testing the SOAP tests

Challenges

Once BPEL processes are deployed into a staging, preproduction, or a production environment, administrators find it difficult to track the health of these key processes. There is a paucity of tools and operational skills in the BPEL area, so it becomes difficult to understand where to look, and what to look for, when faced with a problem. These processes frequently are the automated representation of critical business functions, and they are required to work as expected. Each process could spawn hundreds or thousands of instances daily. If any process is not performing as expected, in terms of availability or performance, the administrators need to step in and resolve the problem. Administrators are required to fix problems as soon as possible, and typically spend most time triaging the problem to understand potential root causes. Further, in most cases, end users report these problems, whether they are consumers via the Internet or key business partners. If that is the case, the enterprise has already lost revenue or credibility, or both.

Solution

Grid Control provides means to monitor critical BPEL processes, partner links, and Web services, through service tests to determine availability and response time. Grid Control also provides a means of measuring critical metrics for actual requests initiated against each of the Web services deployed on the container. Grid Control can determine the service availability of all monitored services by utilizing its active end-user monitoring capabilities.

Step-by-step exercises

This set of step-by-step exercises will walkthrough the discovery of a BPEL process home page, and setting up monitoring for the process and partner links.

Navigating to the BPEL PM target home page

Grid Control can monitor several types of targets. The first task is to get to the BPEL PM target home page. All the BPEL-specific monitoring views can be viewed from the target home page.

1. Navigate to the Grid Control home page.
2. In the **Target Search** region on the right, click on the **Search** dropdown.
3. Scroll down to locate and click on the **BPEL Process Manager target** type.
4. Click on the **Go** button.
5. A list of discovered BPEL Process Manager targets is displayed. Click on the one target name of choice. This takes you to the BPEL PM target home page.

If a single BPEL Process Manager target is discovered, the **Go** button will automatically take you to that target's home page.

Navigating to the BPEL process home page

The BPEL target home page is mainly an infrastructure view. There is a section within the target home page to view the list of BPEL processes and their monitoring metrics.

1. From the BPEL target home page, click on the **Processes** tab.

 All the BPEL processes deployed on the server are discovered and displayed here. Note that the processes are displayed within the domain they are deployed in. Summary throughput process instance information is also displayed in the table. These metrics are gathered by default from the BPEL PM server at a preset polling frequency (collection interval). One can easily change the default polling frequency, as well as set thresholds for these out-of-the-box metrics so that alerts and notifications (with notification rules) can be fired.

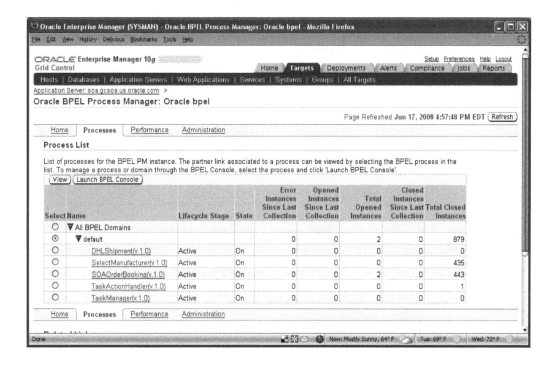

3. Click on the BPEL process name under the default domain, for example **SOAOrderBooking(v1.0)**.

This is the individual BPEL process page. Note the process-specific instance throughput graph. At the bottom, note that all the partner links (at the bottom) for the BPEL process are discovered along with the port type, operation, and WSDL information.

Create the BPEL process aggregate service. Note that you need to create the BPEL Infrastructure Service before you attempt to create the BPEL process aggregate service. Instructions on doing this are provided in *Chapter 4*.

4. From the BPEL process page, click on the **Create Service** button, as shown in the following screenshot:

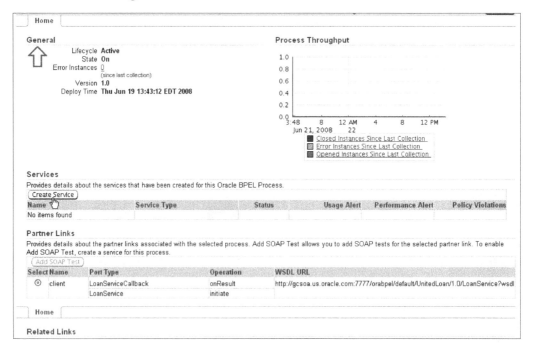

5. Observe the confirmation message for the aggregate service creation.

The aggregate service that was created is listed under the **Services** section. The previously created infrastructure service has automatically been associated with the aggregate service. In the **Services** section, starting from the left, you see the service name, type of service, status, and other alerts. The top-level service is the aggregate service. The next service is the infrastructure service—a subservice of the aggregate.

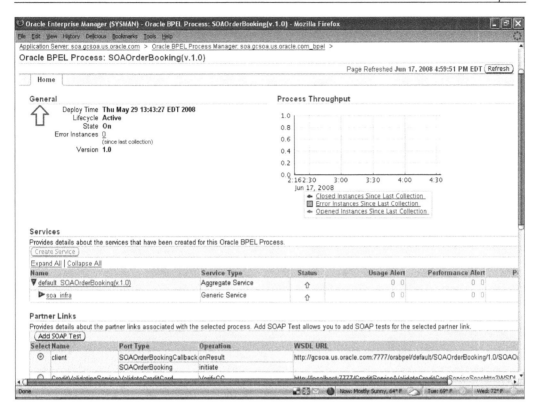

Creating a SOAP test to monitor a partner link

A synthetic transaction is a proactive way to emulate end user (or client) behavior and catch problems before the end user (or client). A BPEL process typically invokes one or more web services through a partner link framework, usually via SOAP. A synthetic check for testing the BPEL partner link availability and performance is a great way to uncover problems before the service consumers do.

1. Scroll down and select a partner link name from the radio button list, for instance, **SelectService**.

2. Click on the **Add SOAP Test** button to create a SOAP test for that partner link.

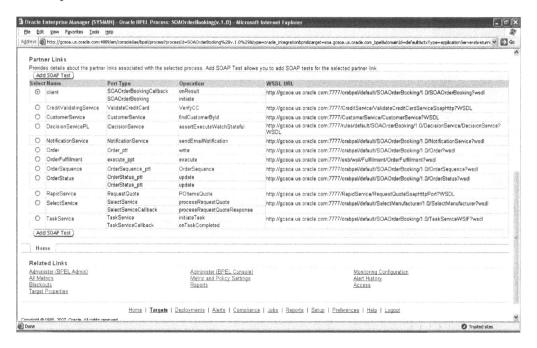

3. Enter the **SOAP Test Name** as **SelectService_test.**

4. Enter the test interval for the **Collection Frequency (minutes)** as **15.**

5. Select Web service port from the **Port Types** drop-down list as **SelectServiceCallbackPort.**

6. Enter input parameters in the HTML input fields, for example, **SupplierPrice {String}** as **12345** and **SupplierName {String}** as **2.**

7. Leave the **Basic Authentication Credentials** section empty.

8. Click on **OK** to continue after the fields on the **Create SOAP Test** page are filled as shown in the following screenshot:

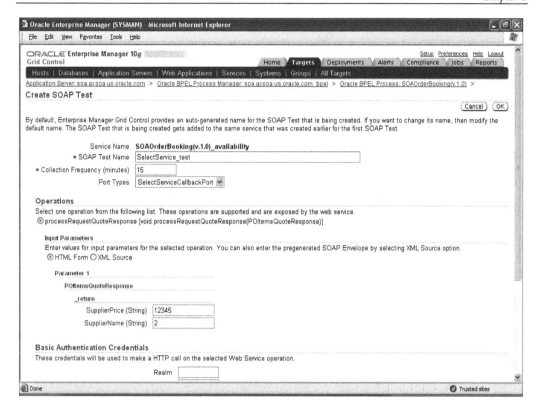

9. Add a beacon. Click on the **Add** button.

10. From the pop-up window, check and select the available beacon(s), shown in the next screenshot:

Beacons are agents that have been configured to issue synthetic tests to test websites, Web services, mail servers, FTP sites, and so on. A beacon is typically installed outside the firewall from a location where users access the website or Web service. A beacon thus "emulates" end user behavior and informs the administrator proactively about any problem with the website or Web service. You can read more about beacons and service management in the Grid Control documentation on the Oracle Technology Network—http://otn.oracle.com.

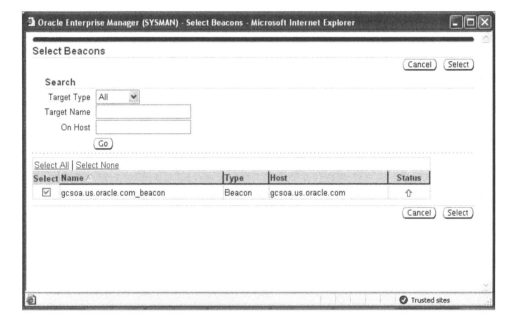

11. Click on **OK** to save the SOAP test and beacon settings.

12. Verify availability process creation and view SOAP test. On the BPEL process home page, note the availability Generic Service that was automatically created.

13. Expand the process availability service. For example, **SOAOrderBooking(v1.0)_availability** and verify that the SOAP test that you just created, for example **SelectService_test**, has been added.

 The availability service for the BPEL process is formed when the first SOAP test is created. Note the status of each test, and how it is rolled up (configurable) to determine process availability. The status of the SOAP test will take some time to show up, based on the frequency set for the test.

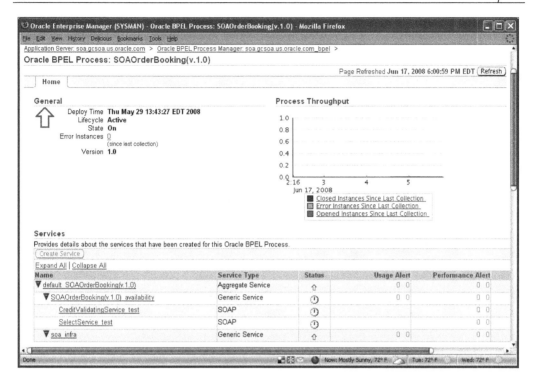

Creating a SOAP test to monitor a BPEL process

Similar to monitoring partner links through synthetic checks, the overall BPEL process can also be monitored in the same manner. A BPEL process is typically invoked by a SOAP client. This can be tested at a desired frequency to ensure that the BPEL process can be instantiated at all times by clients:

1. Go to the BPEL process home page.

2. Scroll down and locate the radio button for **client** in the **Partner Links** section.

3. Click on **Add SOAP Test** to create a SOAP test for the client, as shown in the following screenshot:

4. Select the desired port type as **SOAOrderBookingPort.**

5. Select the radio button for the input parameters as **XML Source.**

6. Enter the SOAP envelope, including any headers. You can copy this SOAP envelope from existing BPEL instances (from the BPEL Control). Copy and paste the SOAP payload provided in the input XML source.

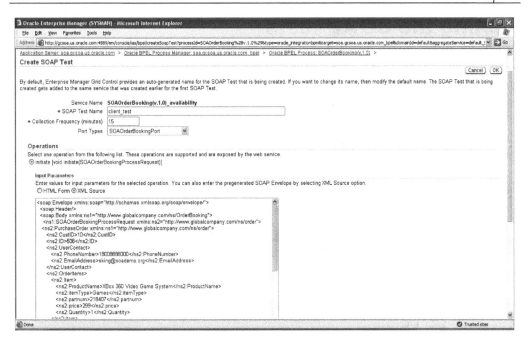

7. Click on **OK** to complete the creation of the client test.

8. Observe the confirmation message.

9. Expand the availability service to view the SOAP tests.

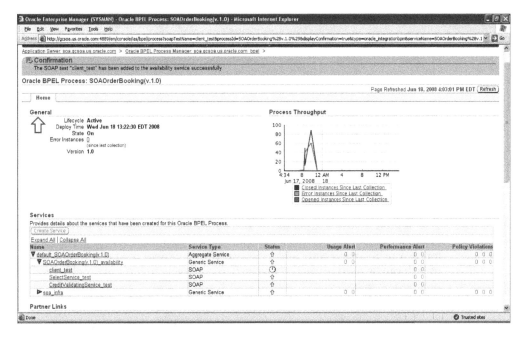

Testing the SOAP tests

There should be a way to track the historical availability and performance of SOAP tests and alert on any deviation from normal behavior via thresholds. When an alert is fired, the on-call person must test whether the reported problem is still in effect. Instantaneous on-demand testing is a great way to achieve this goal.

1. Click on one of the SOAP tests that you created. The test page shows the test availability, beacons that run this test, and alerts associated with this test. The following graph shows the test response times from the beacon:

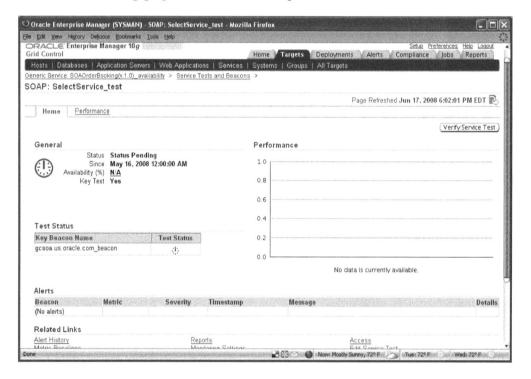

2. Click on the **Verify Service Test** button.

3. Click on the **Perform Test** to run the test instantaneously and view the results.

 One or more beacons could be used to test the service, potentially from multiple geographic locations that emulate the user base. This is useful for measuring availability and response time as experienced by the end user. It can be used proactively as well as reactively to replicate problems reported by users.

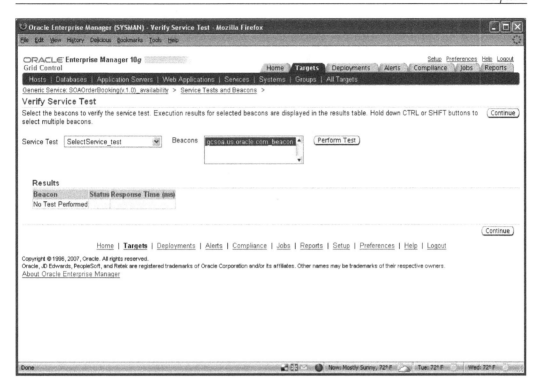

This concludes the step-by-step exercises to set up and view monitoring of BPEL processes from Grid Control.

Summary

Monitoring is key to guaranteeing the health of key business processes in the enterprise. In this chapter, we looked at how to monitor partner links and BPEL processes using synthetic tests. In particular, we looked at challenges related to monitoring BPEL processes, and the solutions provided by Grid Control.

We looked at the basic BPEL process monitoring provided out of the box. Further, we were able to set up specific proactive checks to test the availability and performance of BPEL processes. These synthetic checks had the ability to notify the administrator based on preset thresholds. Further the administrator had the capability to run these synthetic checks on-demand and view the results.

Proactive monitoring can avoid loss of credibility with end users who interact with these business processes. Sometimes everything might be working fine within the firewall, but end users are still unable to access these processes. In this scenario, it is imperative to have an agent sitting outside the firewall to ensure that user behavior can be replicated frequently, and administrators can be notified. In most cases, these agents notify the administrators before end users.

The next chapter will walkthrough hands-on exercises to set up and perform additional management tasks for the BPEL infrastructure, such as the BPEL Process Manager Server, application server, database, and host.

4
BPEL Infrastructure
Management

BPEL installations involve several pieces of software. For a basic single node installation, there are four components. The first one is the dehydration database that persists the BPEL metadata and the BPEL instance information, including instances that are currently being executed ("in-flight" instances). The second component is the application server that provides the platform for BPEL. BPEL is supported on Oracle WebLogic Server, Oracle Application Server, IBM WebSphere, and JBoss. The application server consists of various components such as a **Java Virtual Machine (JVM)** and a web server. The latest certification of application server platform listing can be found here:

```
http://www.oracle.com/technology/software/products/ias/files/oracle_
soa_certification_101310.html.
```

The third component is the BPEL PM server itself, which is fundamentally a Java application. This application is packaged with the Oracle Application Server as part of the SOA Suite installation. The last component is the hardware server and the operating system that hosts the application server and database.

Being an integration product, BPEL orchestrates services that reside on other infrastructure (different from its own infrastructure). This creates a nightmare for the administrators who are tasked with supporting BPEL orchestrations and failures associated with them.

Monitoring the BPEL and the extended infrastructure is important for IT to maintain visibility, get notified, and resolve problems quickly. This chapter talks about managing the BPEL infrastructure by monitoring, viewing configuration changes, and best practice policy violations. Specifically, this chapter talks about:

- Challenges
- Solution
- Step-by-step exercises:
  - Creating the BPEL infrastructure service
  - Viewing the BPEL infrastructure service
  - Viewing system alerts and policies
  - Viewing configuration changes
  - Viewing key system metrics
  - Viewing administration tasks
  - Viewing system components
  - Viewing the system dashboard

Challenges

Critical business processes can often go down due to a failure in a dependent infrastructure. Administrators find it hard to manage BPEL infrastructure along with other existing infrastructure systems. As a BPEL process dehydrates by storing state constantly in its database, any outages or performance problems in the database affect BPEL dehydration and rehydration. There are other infrastructure components such as web server, application server, and host that need to be functioning well for BPEL processes to run smoothly. An administrator who does not have BPEL knowledge or training may not understand what the critical infrastructure pieces are or how to manage them. Further best practices associated with the infrastructure components may not be known or difficult to implement. SOX and COBIT standards have become vital for IT administrators to not only be aware of, but also implement and monitor.

Solution

Grid Control monitors the availability of the BPEL infrastructure components. Both current and historic availability of targets (such as BPEL PM server) are recorded for troubleshooting and root cause analysis. The BPEL infrastructure system and service availability is also recorded. Administrators can be notified when any of the components go down, or troubleshoot after the fact via topology maps to understand which component was responsible for the service failure. By allowing administrators to "manage many-as-one", management of large numbers of components is significantly simplified. By combining BPEL-related targets in systems, administrators can benefit from a wealth of system management features, such as ability to proactively monitor availability through the System Monitoring Dashboard. Administrators can view operational best practice policy violations that help with SOX and COBIT compliance.

Step-by-step exercises

This set of step-by-step exercises will walkthrough the discovery of a BPEL process home page, and setting up monitoring for the process and partner links.

Creating the BPEL infrastructure service

Creating a logical representation of the infrastructure components is the first step to set up effective monitoring. Grid Control helps the administrator to understand the relationships between the infrastructure components.

1. From the BPEL target page, click on the **Create BPEL Infrastructure Service** button.

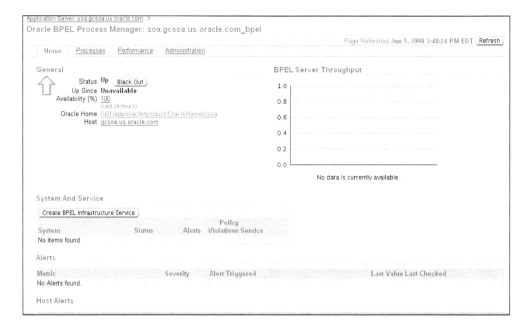

2. On the **Create Service** page, enter a **Service Name** and click on **OK**, as shown in the following screenshot:

3. You should get a confirmation message. Click on **OK**.

 Observe the newly created system and service, status of system and service, alerts, and policy violations.

Viewing the BPEL infrastructure service

Once the infrastructure service has been created, it's useful to view and understand the underlying components of the service.

1. Navigate to the BPEL target home page.
2. Under the **System and Service** section, click on **System**.

 This is the System home page. Notice the pie chart that displays the status of the system components. Notice the alerts, policy violations, and security policy violations on the right. These have been rolled up for all the system components. Observe the services dependent on this system, their status, alerts, violations, and so on. At the bottom, observe the latest configuration changes for the system components.

Viewing system alerts and policies

Grid Control monitors individual system components and tracks all the alerts for the components, as well as different types of policy violations.

1. On the System home page, click on the **Alert History** button. Notice the warning and critical alert history for each system component.

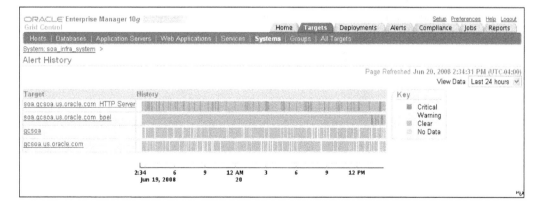

2. Click on the **System** breadcrumb to go back to the System home page.

3. Click on a current **Critical** (red cross) or **Warning** (yellow triangle) number.

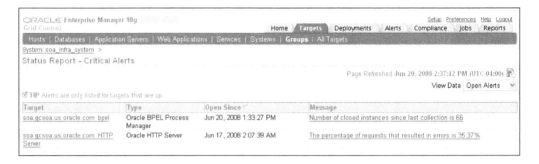

4. Notice the alerts for the different target types. Notice the dropdown to view current alerts as well as historical ones.

5. View Policies (Best Practices) for the system.

 An Enterprise Manager Policy is an operational best practice that ensures proper monitoring of Oracle targets based on Oracle best practices. An example of a database security policy is that the SYSTEM password must be changed every three months. If this is not done, the Agent will flag the database target(s) that violate this policy. There are over 300 policies for database, application server, and applications that are monitored by Grid Control out of the box. With Grid Control 10.2.0.5, custom policies can be added to the library and attached to targets as well.

6. Navigate to the System home page using the breadcrumb.

7. Under **Policy Violations** section, click on the **Violation count**.

8. Notice the different Oracle "best practice" violations for the system components.

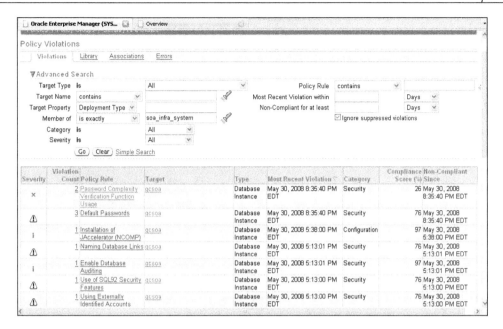

9. Click on a **Policy Rule** to get further information on the "best practice".

10. Use the browser **Back** button twice to navigate to the System home page.

11. Under the **Policy Violations** section, click on **Policy Trend Overview**.

12. Notice the trend overview data for the three policy categories.

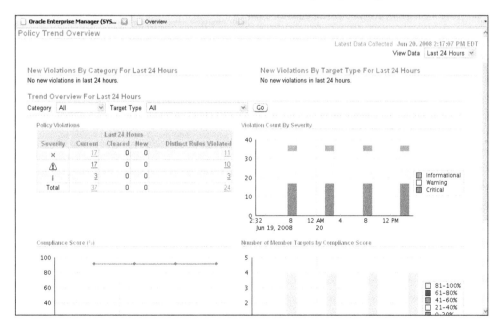

Viewing configuration changes

Grid Control collects configuration information for all its managed targets. This is a great asset for the administrator to understand and troubleshoot problems related to changes in the infrastructure.

1. Click on the *System* breadcrumb to go to the System home page.

2. Under the **Configuration Changes** section, click on **All Target Types**.

3. View the **Configuration History** section for all the system components.

 Notice the changes across all the system components; drill down into specific target types to see the changes. There is a separate chapter on configuration management later.

Viewing key system metrics

Grid Control's default system views capture the key metrics for the system and display it for the administrator.

1. Click on the **Back** button on your web browser to go to the System home page.

2. Click on the **Charts** sub-tab.

 Note the key metrics for the system components graphed on this page. A dropdown is provided to change the time range of the graphs. The set of metrics to display on this page is configurable.

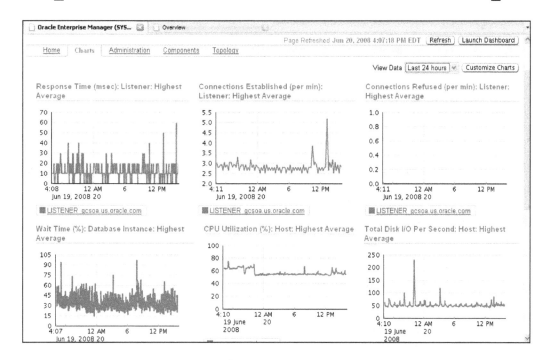

Viewing administration tasks

The administrator can launch several other administrative tasks from Grid Control.

1. Click on the **Administration** tab.

Notice the **Job Activity** for the system components, as well as other administration tasks that can be launched directly from this page.

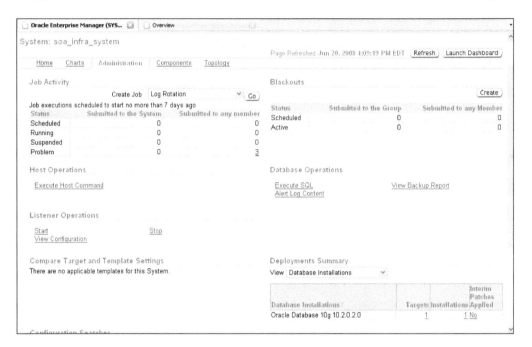

Viewing system components

Viewing the system components lets the administrator figure out what is part of the system, and what affects the overall availability of the system.

1. Click on the **Components** tab.

 This page displays all the components of this system. An "and" or an "or" relationship between the system components availability determines the availability of the system itself.

Viewing the system dashboard

The system dashboard is a useful tool for the network operation center analysts to see the current status of the system components and their key metrics.

1. Click on **Launch Dashboard** on the top right.

The system dashboard displays the status and key metrics of the system components at a glance. If there are any alerts, they are also displayed at the bottom. This is a useful view for an IT Manager who is interested in a summary view of key system components, their status, and downtime information.

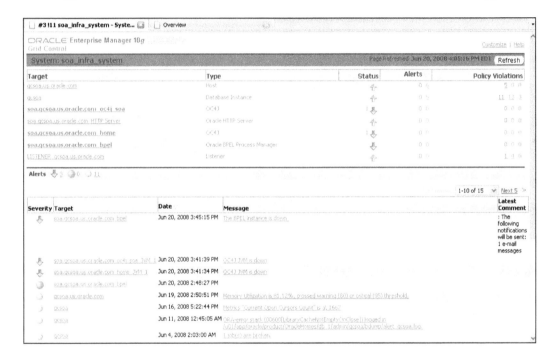

Summary

Monitoring the BPEL infrastructure effectively is essential to the success of SOA projects. Enterprise Manager provides a way to monitor BPEL infrastructure components effectively with existing infrastructure components. We looked at the basic challenges, solution, and step-by-step exercises to address different areas. In particular, we created a BPEL infrastructure service and viewed the service, its underlying system and components, as well as alerts, metrics, and configuration changes. Finally, we viewed the systems components in a system dashboard.

Understanding the key components and creating a system to represent them is the first key step to enabling system management. This allows IT departments to monitor, manage changes, and implement best practice policies to comply with SOX and COBIT standards.

The next few chapters will walkthrough hands-on exercises to set up and perform additional service-level management tasks for the BPEL processes and BPEL infrastructure.

5
BPEL Service-Level Management

Service providers are faced with increasingly demanding consumers who want services that are faster, more available, and perform better. An increasing number of key business services such as e-mail, storage, servers, and databases are used as services, so that consumers do not have to worry about owning and maintaining the software and hardware. Consumers expect high availability and performance regardless of intranet or Internet services. A service downtime could prove detrimental through loss in revenues for the service provider and consumer, and a loss in credibility for both. Further, several service providers have to comply with IT frameworks such as **Information Technology Infrastructure Library (ITIL)**, **Control Objectives for Information and Related Technology (COBIT)**, and **Statement on Auditing Standards 70 (SAS 70)**. These frameworks demand that IT measure service availability and performance for auditing, contractual obligations, and customer satisfaction.

In an environment where services not only abound, but also interact with each other, it becomes a nightmare to govern service availability and quality. A BPEL environment involves several services that are being orchestrated. All the participating services need to be governed within the contractual terms of use. This is extremely important in business to business (or partner) contracts as well as business to consumer contracts. Most service providers have money-back guarantees in contracts that can be invoked by consumers if the quality of service falls beneath mutually agreed availability and performance expectations.

Monitoring BPEL processes and partner links with a common set of service-level expectations is important for IT to monitor service expectations, and resolve problems to ensure service-level agreements are met. This chapter talks about managing the BPEL process and partner link expectations by setting and monitoring service levels. Specifically, this chapter talks about:

- Challenges
- Solution
- Step-by-step exercises:
    - Viewing the BPEL process availability service
    - Adding service performance metrics
    - Setting service-level expectation (availability)
    - Viewing the service availability definition
    - Viewing the BPEL infrastructure service
    - Adding infrastructure performance metrics
    - Adding infrastructure usage metrics
    - Setting service-level expectation (infrastructure)
    - Viewing the infrastructure availability definition
    - Viewing the BPEL process aggregate service
    - Viewing the aggregate service availability definition
    - Adding aggregate service performance and usage metrics
    - Setting service-level expectation (aggregate service)

Challenges

In an increasingly service-oriented environment, service and system availability and response times have a direct and tangible impact on the provider's and consumer's bottom line. BPEL business processes, online banking, online store, and online stock trading are all examples of business applications that need to be monitored and available to partners and end-users. Typically, when any of these services are being used, some common problems faced by the administrators are:

- Guaranteeing availability of a service
- Performance of the service and whether it meets the expectations of the end users

Poor application and infrastructure performance can result in costs to your business, which may include the loss of customer loyalty and sales opportunities.

Solution

Grid Control solves these issues by automatically defining one or more service models that represent the business processes that run in an enterprise. Automated service models overlying business processes are created when one or more service tests (SOAP tests) for partner links are created. Using these service tests (that simulate end-user functionality), administrators can measure the performance and availability of critical partner links or external Web services, receive alerts when there is a problem, identify common issues, and diagnose causes of failures. Monitoring a service helps you ensure that the operational goals and service-level agreements are met.

Step-by-step exercises

This set of step-by-step exercises will walkthrough setting service levels for the BPEL process, and setting up availability and performance metrics to monitor the service levels for the BPEL process and associated availability, infrastructure, and aggregate services. Some key service definitions are listed:

- **Generic Service**: This is a Grid Control representation of any service that is provided to a consumer. There are special services for web applications. For Web services and BPEL processes, the Generic Service is used as a wrapper in order to inherit the Grid Control service capabilities.

- **Availability Service**: This is the representation of a BPEL process in Grid Control to measure the operational availability and response time of the process. Further service level goals can be set and measured at the service level.

- **System**: This is a group of related infrastructure components such as database, application server, JVM, BPEL PM, and so on.

- **Infrastructure Service**: This models the system into a service representation so that service level goals can be set and measured for the overall system.

- **Aggregate Service**: This is a higher-level service that consists of one or more Generic Services.

- **Service-Level Agreement (SLA)**: This is the contractual agreement between a provider and a consumer. Typically, it consists of an availability (for example, 99.99% service uptime per quarter) and performance (for example, Login page should return under three seconds) metrics. Frequently, there are money-back guarantees in the SLA contracts, which can be invoked by the consumer when faced with poor service availability and performance.

- **Service Test**: A Grid Control service can be tested for availability and performance using synthetic checks that emulate end users. As the SLAs are typically measured from a end-user perspective, service tests are extremely useful and used extensively for SLAs.

Viewing the BPEL process availability service

Grid Control creates an internal service representation of a BPEL process automatically. This is useful because normal Grid Control service functionality can be applied. The first step is to navigate to the BPEL process availability service:

1. From the BPEL target page, click on the **BPEL Processes** tab.

2. Click on the BPEL process name `<process_name>` under the default domain, that is, **SOAOrderBooking(v1.0)**.

The Aggregate Service, Availability Service, Generic Service, and the Infrastructure Service may already have been created. If not, please follow the steps in prior chapters to create these services.

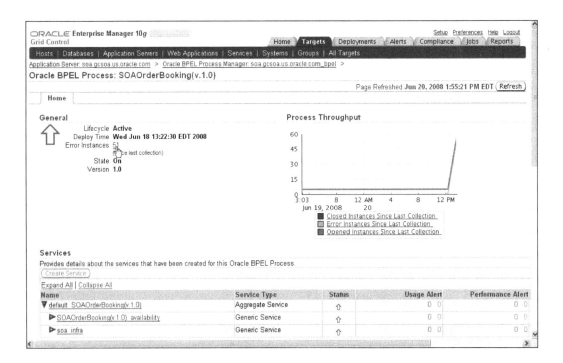

3. Click on the `<process_name_availability>` service name—
   SOAOrderBooking(v1.0)_availability.

 This is the service home page. Notice the **Availability** (%) for the past 24 hours, the **Actual Service Level** (%), and the **Expected Service Level** (%) for this service. Notice the **Key Test Summary** details for this service. The SOAP tests that were instrumented in a prior chapter show up here.

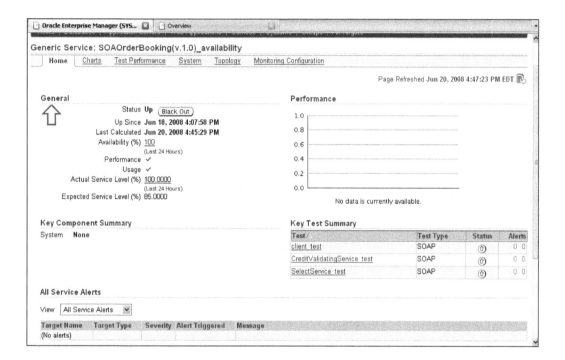

Adding service performance metrics

A Grid Control service can not only be measured on availability but also on performance. Performance metrics such as response time are useful to measure and alert on (based on thresholds), so the operational staff gets alerted before consumers complain.

1. On the service home page, click on **Monitoring Configuration** tab.

2. Click on the **Performance Metrics** link.

3. Add a performance metric **based on service test**, and click on **Go**.

4. For each **Service Test** in the first dropdown, pick the **Response Time (ms)** as metric from the second dropdown, as shown in the following screenshot:

5. Click on **Continue**.

6. Edit the metric name from **Service_Test Response Time (ms)** to **Credit Validating Response Time (ms)**.

7. Enter a **Warning Threshold** and **Critical threshold** time in ms, that is, **3000** and **5000** respectively. Click on **OK**, as shown in the following screenshot:

8. Redo steps 3-7 to add performance metrics for the other service tests' response times if needed.

Setting service-level expectation (availability)

For service providers, Grid Control provides a way to set service-level expectations and measure against those expectations. A service-level expectation can be defined in terms of availability and performance yardsticks over a range of time.

1. From the **Related Links** section at the bottom, click on **Edit Service Level Rule.**

2. Change the **Expected Service Level** from the default value to the value that is required for this service, that is, **99.0**.

3. Observe the default values in the **Actual Service Level** section.

4. Within the **Business Hours** section, change **Start Time** and **End Time** to the required business window that has been discussed with, or is expected by, consumers; for example, **Start Time 08:00** and **End Time 18:00**.

5. Change the default **Availability Criteria** to conform to the business standard. Think about scheduled downtimes (blackout) and whether they are considered as up time for calculations.

6. Under **Performance Criteria**, select one or more metrics from **Available Performance Metrics**.

7. Click on **OK**, as shown in the following screenshot:

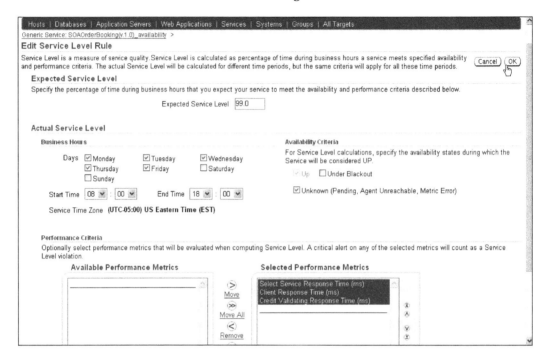

Viewing the service availability definition

The availability definition can be defined based on one or more key tests, such as login test and a response time test. It depends on the contract between provider and consumer. Grid Control is flexible to let the provider code in any formula based on the contractual requirements.

1. Click on the **Monitoring Configuration** tab.

2. Click on **Availability Definition**.

Note the basis for determining availability based on service tests. By default, all service tests are set to "key" service tests. A "key" test is used to determine availability. Non-key test data is also collected historically, but is not used for availability determination.

3. Click on **Cancel**.

Viewing the BPEL infrastructure service

The BPEL infrastructure service encapsulates the infrastructure components that are required for BPEL processes to run.

1. Click on the **Target Services** tab.

2. Locate the infrastructure service (generic service) created in a previous chapter.

3. Click on the infrastructure service to go to the service home page.

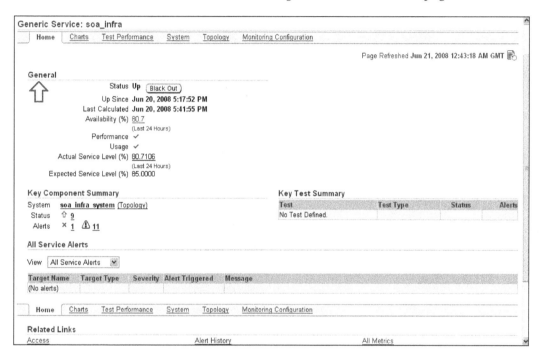

Adding infrastructure performance metrics

Not only are service test metrics important, but infrastructure metrics can also be used to represent service disruptions.

1. Click on the **Monitoring Configuration** tab.

2. Click on the **Performance Metrics** link.

3. As shown in the next screenshot, for the default performance metrics already listed, enter **Warning Threshold** and **Critical Threshold** for some of these metrics as follows :

   ° **OC4J Instance – Request Processing Time (seconds)**: 3 and 5

   ° **Number of Transactions (per second)**: 20 and 50

   ° **Highest number of active threads [default]**: 5 and 10

   ° **CPU Utilization (%)**: 80 and 95

   ° **Average Synchronous Process Latency (msecs) [default]**: 3000 and 5000

   ° **Average Asynchronous Process Latency (msecs) [default]**: 3000 and 5000

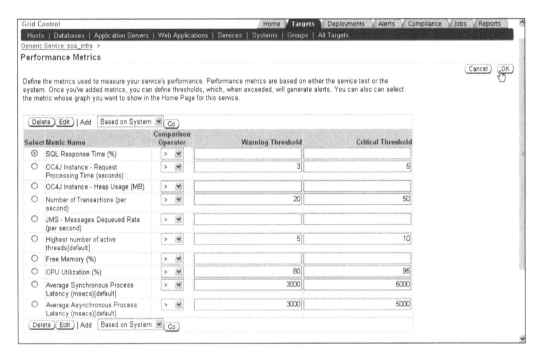

4. Change the chart on home page dropdown to show CPU utilization.

5. Click on **OK** and click on **Yes** on the confirmation screen.

Adding infrastructure usage metrics

Usage metrics are not counted toward availability, but are useful to evaluate the growth of a service. Performance and usage are usually indicators that are viewed side by side.

1. Click on the **Usage Metrics** link.

2. For the default **Usage Metrics** already listed, enter **Warning Threshold** and **Critical Threshold** for some of these metrics as follows:

   ° **Opened Instances Since Last Collection [default]**: 20 and 50

   ° **OC4J Instance – Active Sessions**: 5 and 10

   ° **OC4J Instance – Active Requests**: 20 and 50

   ° **Closed Instances Since Last Collection [default]**: 20 and 50

3. Change the chart on home page dropdown to show **OC4J Instance – Active Requests**, as shown in the following screenshot:

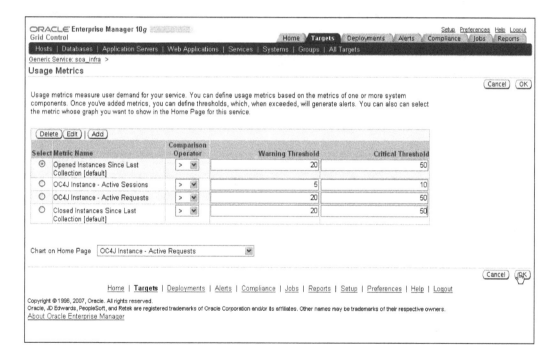

4. Click on **OK** and click on **Yes** on the confirmation screen.

Setting service-level expectation (infrastructure)

Similar to how expectations for a service can be set and measured, an expectation and measurement can also be done for a collection of logical infrastructure components.

1. From the **Related Links** section at the bottom, click on **Edit Service Level Rule**.

2. Change the **Expected Service Level** from the default value to the value that is required for this service, that is, **99.0**.

3. Observe the default values in the **Actual Service Level** section.

4. Within the **Business Hours** section, change the start and end time to the required business window that has been discussed with, or is expected by consumers; for instance, **Start Time** as **08:00** and **End Time** as **18:00.**

5. Change the default **Availability Criteria** to conform to the business standard. Think about scheduled downtimes (blackout) and whether they are considered as up time for calculations.

6. Under **Performance Criteria**, select one or more metrics from **Available Performance Metrics**.

7. Refer to the following screenshot for the preceding steps and click on **OK**.

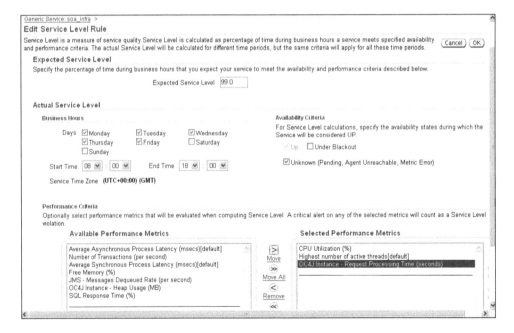

Viewing the infrastructure availability definition

This is similar to viewing the definition for the service availability except the underlying component availability is used to measure availability rather than service tests.

1. Click on the **Monitoring Configuration** tab.

2. Click on the **Availability Definition**.

> Note the basis for determining availability based on system components. By default, all components are set to "key" components. A "key" component is used to determine availability. Non-key component data is also collected historically, but is not used for availability determination.

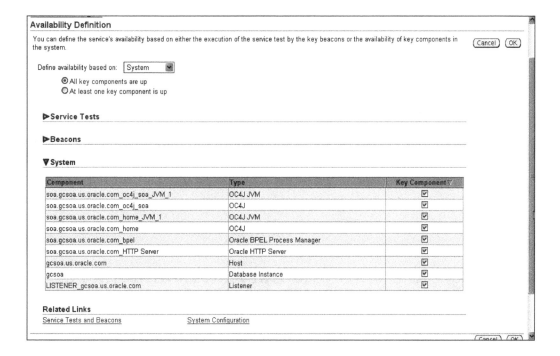

3. Click on **Cancel**.

Viewing the BPEL process aggregate service

The aggregate service is a collection of the availability service and the infrastructure service. When many services are present in the enterprise, this logical grouping makes it easy to view and monitor these services.

1. Click on the **Target | Services** tab.

2. Locate the aggregate service created earlier.

3. Click on the aggregate service to go to the service home page.

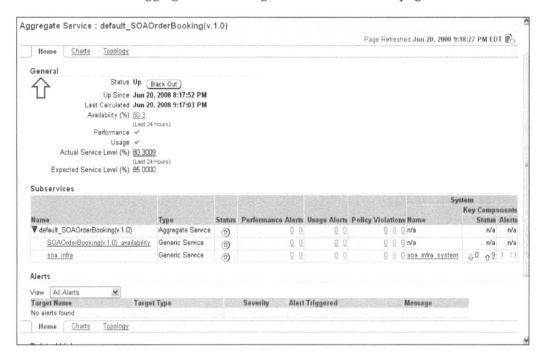

Viewing the aggregate service availability definition

The availability definition for the aggregate service depends on the underlying component services.

1. Under **Related Links** at the bottom, click on **Edit Service**.

 Notice the dependency of this aggregate service on the subservices. Notice the availability definition based on an AND relationship of the two subservices.

Adding aggregate service performance and usage metrics

The underlying service metrics can be promoted to the Aggregate Service level to ensure that the key metrics are visible for network operations control administrators, as well as executives.

1. Click on the **Performance** tab within **Edit Service** mode.

2. Click on the **Add** button to promote subservice metrics.

3. Select the **Based on statistical aggregate from multiple services** option.

4. Set the **Function** dropdown to **Maximum**.

5. Add rows for the **Subservice**, that is, **SOAOrderBooking(v.1.0)_availability (Generic Service)**.

6. Select **Metric Name** for the selected **Subservice** metrics as shown in the following screenshot; for example, **Client Response Time (ms)**, **Select Service Response Time (ms)**, and **Credit Validating Response Time (ms)**.

7. Click on **Continue**.

8. Edit the **Metric Name** to an appropriate name, that is, **Avg BPEL Response Time (ms)**.

9. Enter appropriate warning and critical thresholds; for example, **3000** and **5000**.

10. Add another performance metric. Click on the **Add** button.

11. Select the infrastructure service from the **Subservice** dropdown.

12. Pick a relevant infrastructure metric, that is, **CPU Utilization** (%).

13. Click on **Continue**, as shown in the following screenshot:

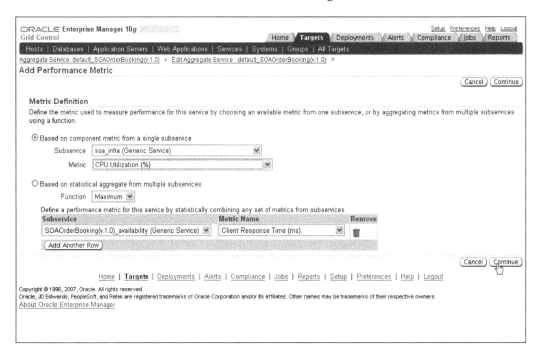

14. Notice that the warning and critical thresholds have been inherited from the subservice. Leave it at the same levels or modify as appropriate.

15. Click on **OK**.

Setting service-level expectation (aggregate service)

This is similar to the expectation that was set for the other services.

1. From the **Related Links** section at the bottom, click on **Edit Service Level Rule**.

2. Change the **Expected Service Level** from the default value to the value that is required for this service, for instance, **99.0**.

3. Observe the default values in the **Actual Service Level** section.

4. Within **Business Hours** section, change start and end time to the required business window that has been discussed with, or is expected by consumers, that is, **Start Time** as **08:00** and **End Time** as **18:00**.

5. Change the default **Availability Criteria** to conform to the business standard. Think about scheduled downtimes (blackout) and whether they are considered as up time for calculations.

6. Under **Performance Criteria**, select one or more metrics from **Available Performance Metrics**.

7. Click on **OK**, as shown in the following screenshot:

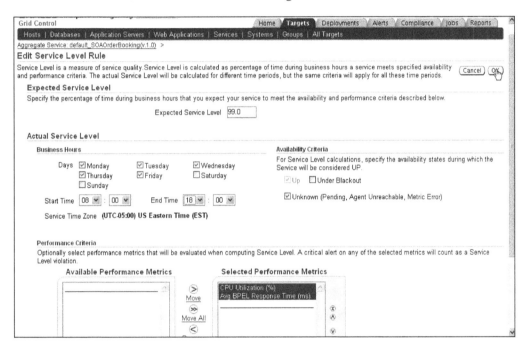

8. From the aggregate service home page, click on the **Charts** tab.

 Notice the promoted performance metrics tracked in charts on this page with the thresholds displayed on the charts.

Summary

Monitoring BPEL services effectively is essential in monitoring consumer expectations and maintaining credibility. Grid Control provides a way to monitor BPEL services effectively with infrastructure services, and their associations.

In this chapter, we discussed how Grid Control sets up the service model around a BPEL process and the BPEL infrastructure. The inbuilt service-level expectation and measurement using availability and performance metrics makes it easy to monitor these services. Further, the metrics can be based on service tests or on infrastructure metrics.

Associating the key service components with infrastructure components, and monitoring them from one integrated view is critical for administrators to set and control consumer expectations.

The next few chapters will walkthrough hands-on exercises to set up service dashboards to monitor the services that have been configured for the enterprise.

6
BPEL Services Dashboard

Most IT departments have a service desk or help desk that acts as the single point of contact for customers. The service desk team is responsible for being the first line of communication to log customer-reported incidents. The service desk analyst is responsible for logging customer incidents, verifying service health and availability, and notifying respective IT departments about new issues.

BPEL processes frequently are responsible for key business functions such as billing, expense reports, and order fulfillment. For company-wide services, the service desk needs to keep track of these critical processes. When users call the service desk to complain about these processes, the analyst needs to look at a common dashboard to verify the status of each process. The analyst needs to understand how long the process has been unavailable or non-performant, and whether the preset **Service Level Agreements (SLAs)** have been violated. They need to take swift action to ensure new incidents are logged and rectified quickly by the IT administrator. This chapter talks about creating a dashboard to monitor critical BPEL processes and monitoring key metrics and SLAs for each process. Specifically, this chapter talks about:

- Challenges
- Solution
- Step-by-step exercises:
    - ° Navigating to the **Reports** tab
    - ° Creating an SOA services dashboard
    - ° Viewing the SOA services dashboard

Challenges

A service desk needs a common dashboard to monitor key BPEL processes. Lack of an effective dashboard in most enterprises translates to poor communication between service providers and consumers. Further, without a common dashboard, SLAs cannot be monitored effectively. The lack of transparency leads to lack of trust and the provider's credibility is affected, even though the process availability and performance fall in line with SLAs.

Solution

Grid Control displays the availability and key metrics for the key services via service dashboards. Service desk analysts, IT administrators, as well as IT executives can keep track of current and historic service levels, by using these dashboards. The top-down service dashboards enable IT organizations to manage from an end-user service perspective. Managing by exception enables support staff to drill down into problem services to determine the root cause of failure before customer complaints or before SLA violations.

Step-by-step exercises

This set of step-by-step exercises will walkthrough creating a service dashboard to monitor critical BPEL processes.

Navigating to the Reports tab

Grid Control has the ability to create, publish, and view standard and custom reports. These reports serve as a window to the monitoring and configuration data stored in the Grid Control repository.

1. From the Grid Control home page, click on the **Reports** tab.
2. Search for **Services Monitoring Dashboard**.

 Grid Control provides several out-of-the-box reports for monitoring, security, and compliance. These reports are complements by service dashboards that can be used by the service desk to monitor key services.

Creating an SOA services dashboard

A dashboard is one of many types of reports. Like other Grid Control reports, there are many configurable aspects, such as the source or target(s), what is to be displayed, and the time period for which the display is to be presented. Dashboards can be displayed in different time zones, have an auto-refresh capability, and the ability to display one or more interesting time windows, such as last day, last week, and last month.

1. Select the radio button next to **Services Monitoring Dashboard**.

2. Click on **Create Like**, as shown in the following screenshot:

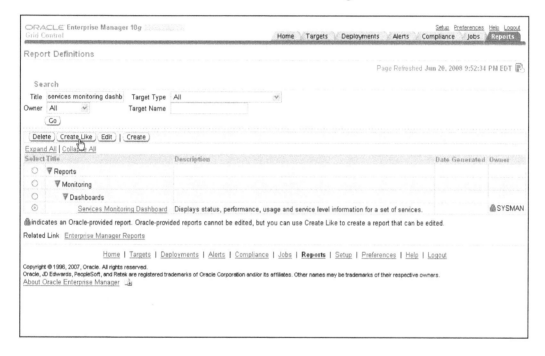

3. Enter **Title** as **SOA Services Dashboard**.

4. Leave the other fields at the defaults.

5. As shown in the following screenshot, under the **Targets** section, select the **Use the specified target** radio button.

6. Click on the **Elements** tab.

7. Click on **Set Parameters**.

8. Edit the header to be **SOA Services Dashboard**.

9. Change the time zone relevant to your geographic location. For example, **(UTC-08:00) US Pacific Time (PST)**.

10. In the **Services** section, pick all the SOA-related services (except EM service).

11. Move the **default_SOAOrderBooking(v.1.0)** aggregate service to the top of the selected list, as shown in the following screenshot:

12. Click on **Continue.**

13. Click on **OK** to save the dashboard settings.

Viewing the SOA services dashboard

Once the dashboard has been created, you can view it and look at the status and health of key services. There are red, yellow, and green indicators for each service, which gives a good bird's eye view of all the services.

1. Navigate to the **Reports** tab.

2. Search for the title **SOA** and click on **Go**.

3. Click on the **SOA Services Dashboard** link.

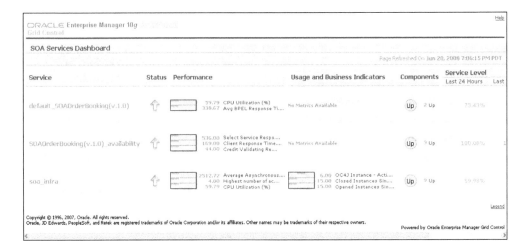

[View all the performance and usage metrics for the
key SOA services. The services dashboard can be
customized to meet the needs of system administrators.]

4. Click on the arrow for the **SOAOrderBooking(v.1.0)_availability**. Expand
   the availability service to view the underlying service tests and their
   individual availabilities.

5. Click on **Back**, to go back to the SOA services dashboard. Click on the arrow for the infrastructure service. Notice all the components, and rolled-up statistics for the components.

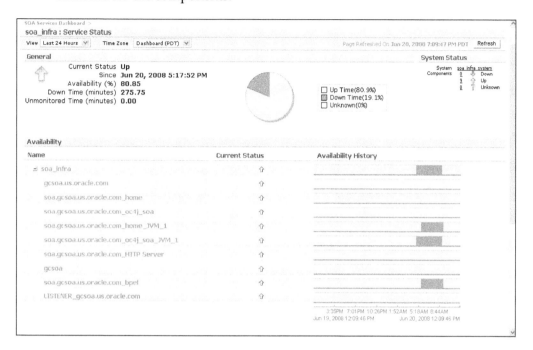

Summary

Service dashboards are essential to any organization that provides services to internal or external consumers. Grid Control lets service desk analysts, IT administrators, and IT executives visualize key service aspects via service dashboards.

In this chapter, we discussed the value of reports as a visualization tool for configuring and monitoring data. We created a new dashboard with the key SOA services, and then viewed the dashboard to look at the status and health of the services.

Note that these service dashboards can be made public for all employees to view a common source for the health and availability of services. This is common for large enterprises for viewing the state of e-mail services, ERP and CRM services, and critical BPEL processes. This is akin to a procedural justice method where the providers and consumers are aware of the common SLA goals, and the level of compliance with those goals.

The next few chapters will walkthrough hands-on exercises to deploy BPEL processes and manage configurations for the BPEL environment.

7
BPEL Deployment Automation

In most medium to large enterprises, application developers write code, and throw it "over the wall" to the operations group. The operations group is now responsible for deploying and maintaining this code in stage and production environments. The development and operations teams typically roll up to separate management chains, and there is little coordination between the two teams.

BPEL process development and deployment follow the same methodology. Administrators have to deal with multiple BPEL process "suitcases", which might be dependent on each other. Typically, the BPEL process deployment should follow the existing methodology in the enterprise. The operational team should centrally maintain the deployment artifacts, and this should be in a different location than the one used by the development team. The deployment itself should be a well-defined procedure with a series of repeatable steps. Further, the set of enterprise best practices should be invoked at deployment time. This chapter talks about deploying multiple BPEL process suitcases to multiple BPEL environments in a standardized manner. Specifically, this chapter talks about:

- Challenges
- Solution
- Step-by-step exercises:
    - ° Viewing the Software Library
    - ° Uploading BPEL suitcases to the Software Library
    - ° Viewing the BPEL process provisioning deployment procedure
    - ° Scheduling BPEL suitcase deployment
    - ° Viewing the status of the scheduled deployment
    - ° Viewing the deployed processes

Challenges

Deploying applications in production environments is a challenge. Administrators have to deploy multiple application files to multiple targets, in a fixed time window. This consumes time and requires expertise on these applications. In a BPEL environment, this is even more challenging when administrators have to deal with *ant scripts* to deploy BPEL suitcases in production environments manually. *Ant* is a great utility for developers when they deal with deployment on developer machines, but administrators do not really have the expertise to customize or build utilities for production-level deployment. Controlling the suitcases centrally is the first challenge, where administrators have to track the suitcases to comply with change and release management guidelines. Next, the deployment itself is a challenge, considering the administrator needs to deploy the processes in a specified order, invoke any custom scripts that might be required, and honor the scheduled maintenance window.

Solution

With Grid Control, administrators can deploy multiple BPEL process suitcases to multiple BPEL PM domains using the Software Library and deployment procedure framework. The administrators' task of gathering deployment information is made simple by Grid Control, which has already discovered the target and knows most of the key properties for the target, such as hostname, application server name, port, and so on. The first step is to upload the BPEL process suitcases into the Software Library for central tracking and deployment. The Software Library also lets the operational team track the maturity and usage of the suitcases, along with other software components, such as operations system images, database, and application server homes. Then, a five-step interview process lets the user pick the source suitcase files, pick the target BPEL PM and domain, set the credentials, and schedule a future deployment using the job system.

Step-by-step exercises

This set of step-by-step exercises will walkthrough uploading and deploying BPEL process suitcases.

Viewing the Software Library

The Grid Control Software Library is a runtime version control system. After developers are done developing the business processes, the artifacts can be passed on to (or read by) the Software Library for operational tracking and deployment.

1. From the Grid Control home page, click on the **Deployments** tab.

2. Click on the **Provisioning** sub-tab.

3. Expand **Components** to reveal the different component types.

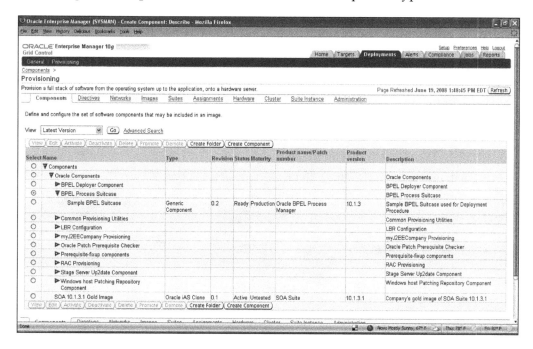

The Software Library contains several objects such as operating system images, Oracle homes for database and application server, deployment artifacts for BPEL, and so on. The library is used to track the maturity of these components as they are used on various monitored targets.

4. Expand **Oracle Component | BPEL Process Suitcase.**

A BPEL suitcase is a BPEL process deployment unit. It is a `jar` file that encapsulates all the components for a BPEL process such as `.bpel`, one or more `.xsd`, and one or more `.wsdl` files.

5. View the sample BPEL suitcase that is part of the Software Library.

Uploading BPEL suitcases to the Software Library

BPEL process projects are packaged into a "BPEL suitcase", which is a self-contained deployment artifact. This artifact can be used by the administrator to deploy to various environments.

1. Select the radio button for **BPEL Process Suitcase**.

2. Click on the **Create Component** button.

3. Enter the following values in the **Describe** step:
   - Select **Type** as **Generic Component**.
   - Name as **ParallelFlow**.
   - Description as **Parallel Flow Sample**.
   - Leave the other fields blank.

4. Click on **Next**, as shown in the following screenshot:

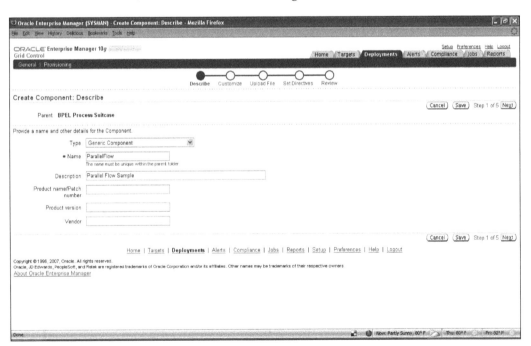

5. In the **Customize** step, leave the defaults and click on **Next**.

6. In the **Upload File** step:
    ◦   Select **Upload from Local Machine**.
    ◦   Click on the **Browse...** button.
    ◦   Locate the BPEL suitcase `jar` file folder.
    ◦   Select `bpel_parallel_flow.jar` for the current example.

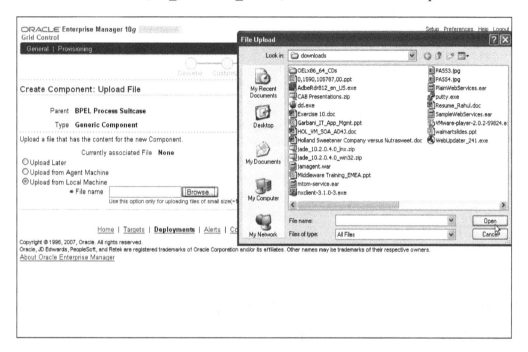

7. Click on **Next**.
8. In the **Set Directives** step, select **Stage** and click on **Next**.
9. In the **Review** step, note the details, and click on **Finish**.
10. Note the confirmation message, and the new BPEL suitcase added.

11. Repeat the preceding steps to add additional BPEL suitcases to the Software Library.

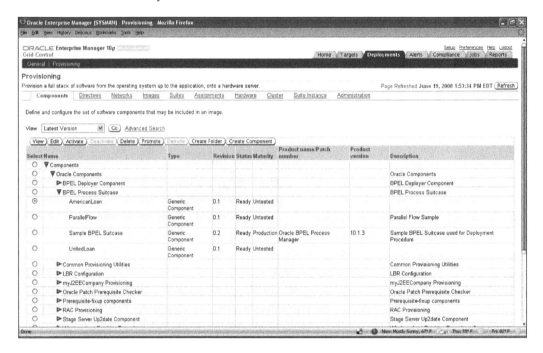

Viewing the BPEL process provisioning deployment procedure

Grid Control consists of several deployment procedures that are used to automate various administrative activities.

1. From the Grid Control home page, click on the **Deployments** tab.

2. Scroll down to locate the **Deployment Procedure Manager** section.

3. Click on the **Deployment Procedures** link.

 A deployment procedure is a series of logical steps that automate key administrative tasks related to Oracle products. Most of these complex administrative tasks are listed in the "Enterprise Deployment Guide". Note the various deployment procedures available out of the box—database provisioning, RAC extend, application server provisioning, and so on. These deployment procedures can be customized as well.

4. Click on the **BPEL Process Provisioning** link.

5. Note the steps underlying the procedure:

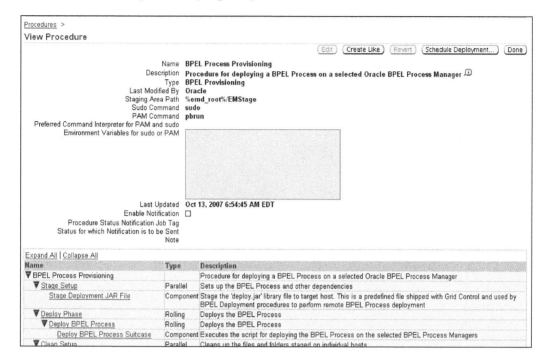

Scheduling BPEL suitcase deployment

The primary task for the administrator is to schedule the out-of-the-box deployment procedure to run once, or to a schedule.

1. Continuing from the previous step, click on the **Schedule Deployment** button.

2. In the **Source Selection** step:

    °   Click on **Add** to select the source suitcase bundles.

 These bundles are stored in the Grid Control Software Library before actual deployment.

- From the existing suitcases, you can select one or more to deploy. For example, select **ParallelFlow**, **UnitedLoan**, and **AmericanLoan**.

- Click on **Select** to continue.

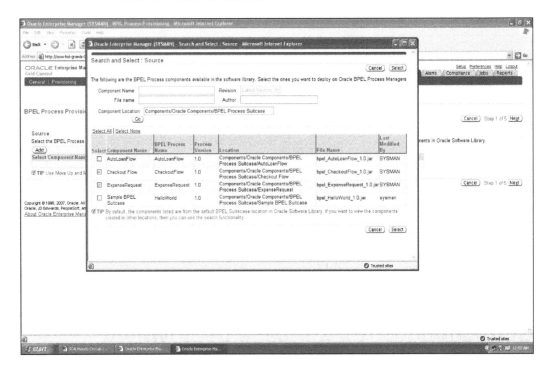

- Use the **Move Up** and the **Move Down** buttons to order the deployment.

 Order of deployment is essential in a BPEL environment, where partner links are typically deployed before the BPEL Process that invokes them.

- Click on **Next** to continue.

3. In the **Target Selection** step, follow these steps as shown in the next screenshot:

- Click on **Add** to select one or more targets from the list of managed BPEL targets; for example, select **gcsoa.us.oracle. com_bpel**.

- Click on **Select** to continue.

- ○ Select **default** from the **BPEL Domain** dropdown for each BPEL target.
- ○ Click on **Next** to proceed, as shown in the following screenshot:

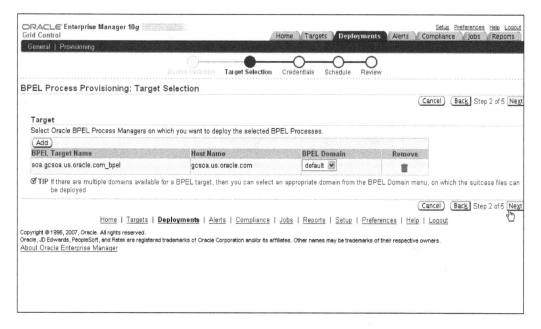

4. In the **Credentials** step, follow these steps as shown in the next screenshot:
   - ○ Provide the credentials for the host under **Application Server Credentials**; that is, **Username** as **oracle and Password as** *welcome1*.
   - ○ Click on **Next** to proceed.
   - ○ Under **BPEL Process Manager Credentials**, provide domain level access; that is, **Username** as **oc4jadmin** and **Password** as *welcome1*.

These credentials for host and BPEL Process Manager can be stored in the Grid Control "Preferred Credentials" page and reused.

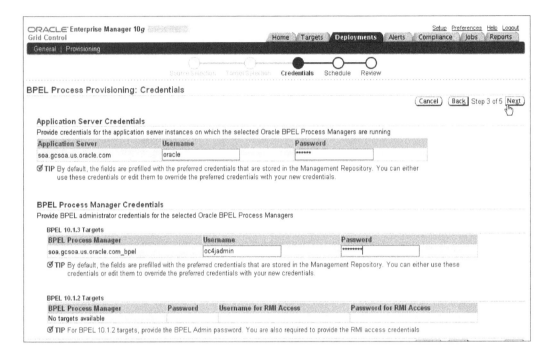

- ° Click on **Next**.

5. In the **Schedule** step, follow these steps as shown in the next screenshot:

    - ° Click on **One Time (Later)** and select a **Start Date** (for example, **June 23, 2008**) and **Start Time** can be anything from a couple of minutes later.

    - ° Enter **BPEL Process Provisioning** for the **Instance Name** field.

    - ° Click on **Next** to proceed, as shown in the next screenshot:

Deployment can be scheduled immediately or for a future time, typically during a customer maintenance window. The Grid Control job system takes care of the job scheduling and management.

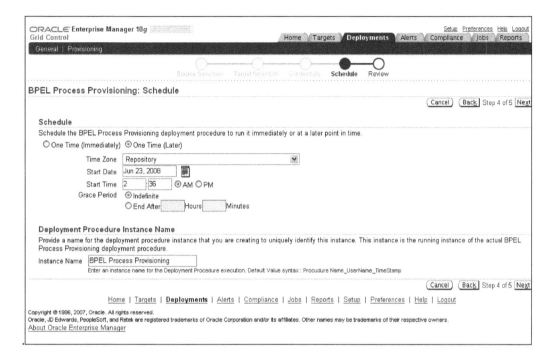

6. In the **Review** step:

   ° Review all the information before submitting a deployment job.

- ° Click on **Finish** when you're ready, as shown in the following screenshot:

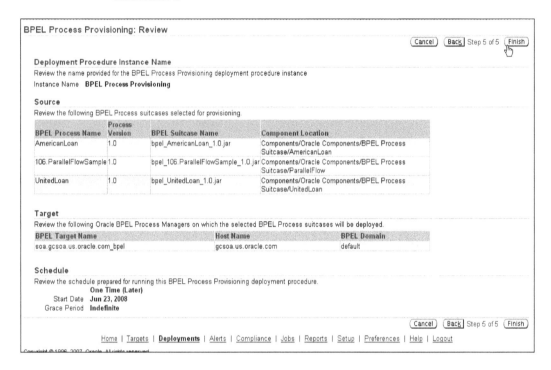

Viewing the status of the scheduled deployment

Grid Control provides means to observe the overall deployment status and individual step status from its jobs page.

1. Continuing from the previous step, find the **BPEL Process Provisioning** job from the **Procedure Completion Status** tab.

2. Click on the **BPEL Process Provisioning** job to view the details, as shown in the following screenshot:

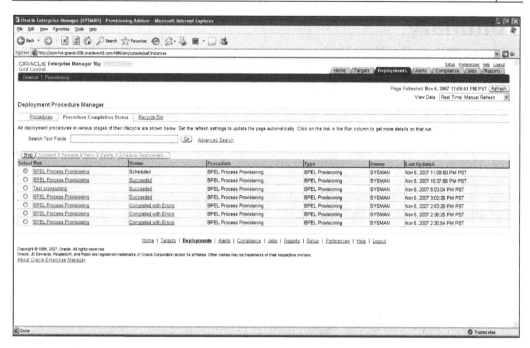

 The job status page shows the details of the scheduled job, including elapsed time and error messages if any.

3. Use the **Refresh** button on the top right to see the progress.

4. Wait for the job to finish successfully.

5. Note the **Status** and **Completed Date** values.

Viewing the deployed processes

Once the deployment has completed successfully, you can verify the new process on the BPEL console:

1. Navigate to the BPEL target home page.

2. Click on the **Processes** tab.

3. Click on the **Refresh** button on the top right.

4. Note the newly deployed processes in the list.

Summary

Deployment is a critical task for operational administrators. With the Grid Control Software Library and deployment procedure capabilities, administrators can manage BPEL suitcases, and schedule and automate deployment.

In this chapter, we discussed how to utilize the out-of-the-box deployment functionality with Grid Control. The administrator can view the deployment procedures, pick the right one, schedule the deploy, and observe the deploy taking place. This is a powerful automation framework that can be utilized for deploying repeatedly and on multiple environments at the same time. There are other variations of these deployments that might be useful, such as running a custom script after the end of the deployment.

With Grid Control release 10gR5, the deployment plan (introduced with BPEL 10.1.3.4) methodology is also supported. In other words, a deployment plan file with details of partner links for test, stage, and production environments can be uploaded to the Software Library. This file can be used while scheduling deployment and the partner link changes will automatically be done. It is also common for customers to create a copy of the out-of-box deployment procedure, and add a few custom steps with home-grown scripts that need to be executed before or after deployment.

The next few chapters will walkthrough hands-on exercises to manage configurations for the BPEL environment.

8
BPEL Configuration Management

Managing the configurations of software and hardware assets in an enterprise is important for several reasons. "Knowing what you have" enables IT managers to make decisions about future investments and retiring old assets, standardize existing assets, manage change across the enterprise, and troubleshoot performance problems related to configurations.

Most configuration management solutions today are compliant with the best practices laid out by the **IT Information Library** (**ITIL**) framework. All the assets are stored in a central repository called the **Configuration Management Database** (**CMDB**). Configuration parameters such as `init.ora` parameters for a database, or `startup` parameters for a WebLogic application server, or port numbers for an HTTP server are stored in the CMDB. Any changes to these parameters are also tracked. It then becomes easy to audit the changes for a specific asset, compare assets to each other (for example database1 and database2), compare different versions of the same asset, save a reference configuration to the CMDB, and use that to standardize across the enterprise. This chapter talks about managing configurations for a BPEL environment. Specifically this chapter talks about:

- Challenges
- Solution
- Step-by-step exercises:
    - Navigating to BPEL target configuration management:
        - Viewing the last collected configuration
        - Saving a configuration snapshot to the repository

- ° Navigating to Oracle Application Server configuration management:
    - Viewing the last collected configuration
    - Saving a configuration snapshot to the repository
- ° Making changes to the BPEL environment
- ° Making changes to the Oracle Application Server environment
- ° Comparing the current BPEL configuration with a saved baseline
- ° Comparing BPEL process versions for the same process
- ° Comparing the current Oracle Application Server configuration with a saved baseline
- ° Viewing application server target comparison results with a saved baseline

Challenges

It is difficult to track the configurations of all IT systems. Frequently, IT departments resort to Excel spreadsheets to store critical IT system information. This makes an IT department slow in making changes, measuring impact, and identifying performance problems due to incorrect configuration, and increases the costs of managing a data center. With a BPEL environment, it is difficult to baseline a working configuration and compare it with non-working ones. There is no good way to compare successive BPEL Process versions before rolling them out into production.

Solution

With Grid Control, key configuration metrics for BPEL PM server and processes are collected and stored in the Grid Control configuration management database. This is the same database repository that houses the monitoring information. Administrators can view the historic configuration changes across the BPEL environment. They can also baseline a working configuration by saving it in the repository. A BPEL PM server and domain's configuration parameters can be compared with other server and domains. Finally, BPEL Process versions can also be compared to observe the changes across successive deployments.

Step-by-step exercises

This set of step-by-step exercises will walkthrough managing configurations for the BPEL and application server targets.

Navigating to BPEL target configuration management

Grid Control has rich configuration management functionality for all its managed targets such as database, application server, BPEL PM, and so on.

1. Navigate to the BPEL target home page.

2. Click on the **Administration** tab.

3. Note the links related to configuration management for the target.

 Grid Control configuration management framework picks up key configuration parameters for BPEL on a daily basis. These parameters are stored in the Grid Control repository. Key configuration tasks can be accessed from here.

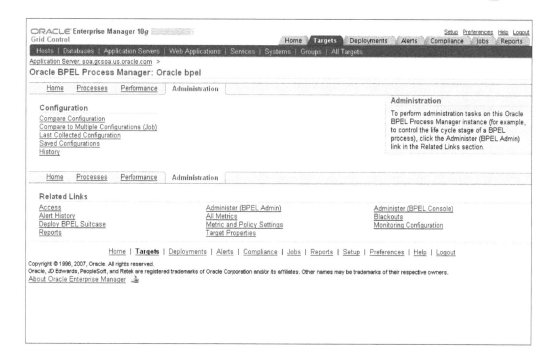

Viewing the last collected configuration

The Grid Control agent collects configuration metrics at a regular interval (default once in 24 hours) and uploads to the configuration management repository. This enables Grid Control to track the configuration history of the managed target. There are several ways to look at the configuration history, one of them being the last collected configuration.

1. Click on **Last Collected Configuration** to view configuration parameters.

2. View the configuration settings on the **Last Collected Configuration** page.

3. The **Process Manager** tab shows generic information about the server including URLs, dehydration store, and cluster parameters.

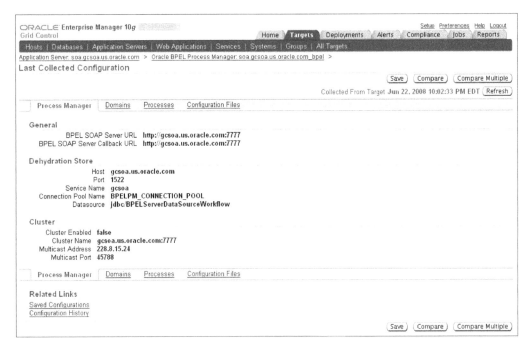

4. Click on the **Domains** sub-tab. The **Domains** tab lists the BPEL domains and important configuration parameters for each domain.

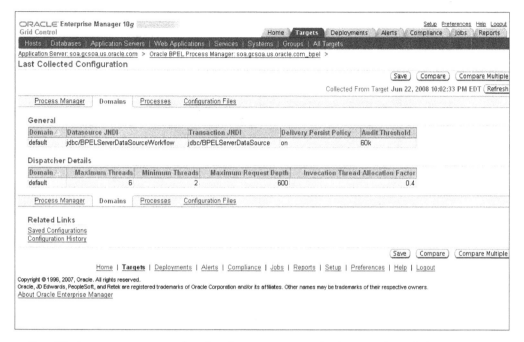

5. Click on **Processes** sub-tab. The **Processes** tab shows a list of deployed processes with version information, underlying files, and last modified time.

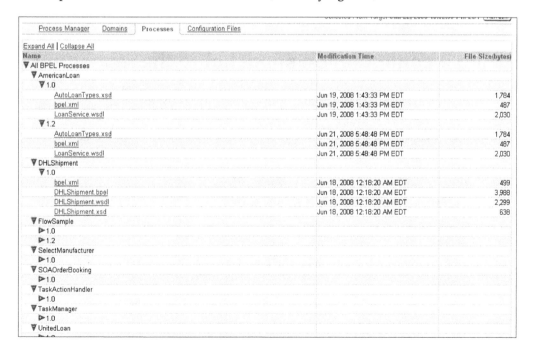

6. Click on **Configuration Files**. Key configuration files from the BPEL server are now stored in the Grid Control repository and displayed on this tab. You can click on the file to view the contents in read-only mode.

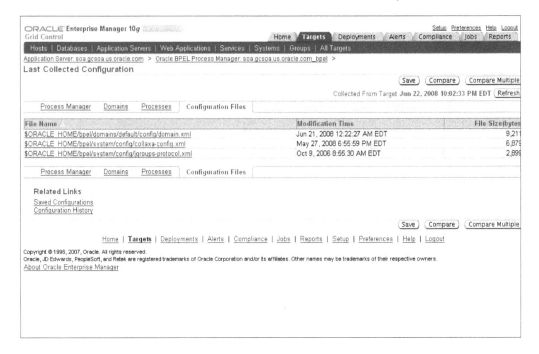

Saving a configuration snapshot to the repository

In a large enterprise it is important to standardize configuration across a target type. This helps in ease of maintenance and is also important for compliance reasons. To standardize configurations, Grid Control provides a way to create a "gold" configuration based on an existing target configuration, and then use that to standardize against other targets:

1. Click on the **Save** button on the top right.
2. Select the option **Save to EM Repository**.

3. Enter a description such as **GCSOA_<date>_BPEL_Baseline**, as shown in the following screenshot:

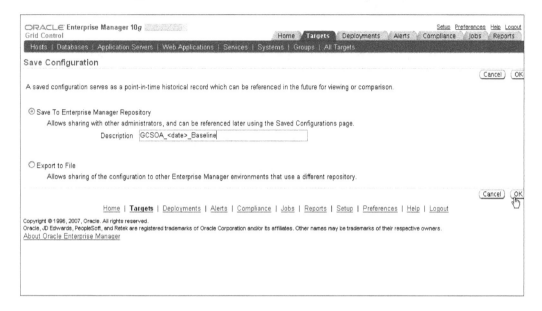

4. Click on **OK** to save the current configuration to the Grid Control repository.

5. Note the confirmation message and the saved configuration with timestamp, name, description, saved date, and owner.

Navigating to Oracle Application Server configuration management

It is useful to look at an Oracle application server configuration as well because BPEL is hosted by the application server:

1. From the Grid Control home page, click on the **Targets** tab.

2. Select the **Application Servers** sub-tab.

3. Click on the name of the application server such as **soa.gcsoa.us.oracle.com**.

4. This takes you to the home page for the application server.

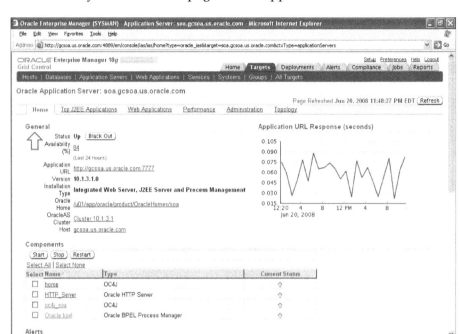

5. Click on the **Administration** tab.

 Grid Control configuration management framework picks up key configuration parameters for all Oracle Application Server targets and individual components (web server, OC4J, BPEL PM, and many more) on a daily basis. These parameters are stored in the Grid Control repository.

Viewing last collected configuration

Often, the first thing the administrators want to see is the current configuration of a target. This typically corresponds to the "last collected configuration" in Grid Control, and can be refreshed to initiate an on-demand collection for up-to-date information.

1. Select the **Last Collected Configuration** link, as shown in the following screenshot:

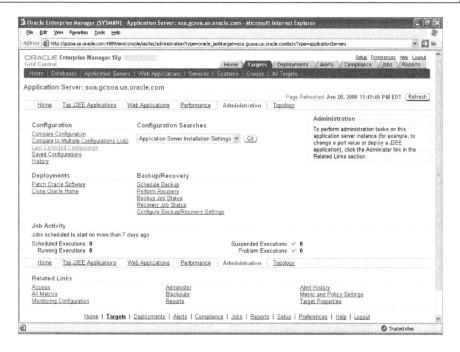

2. The current configuration of the application server is displayed. The **General** tab displays key components of the application server and also some key configuration parameters, as shown in the following screenshot:

3. Click on the **J2EE Applications** tab to view all the J2EE applications deployed on this application server.

4. Click on the **Configuration Files** tab to view the key configuration files. You can click on the files to view a read-only version of the files.

Saving a configuration snapshot to the repository

Similar to the BPEL configuration snapshot, the application server configuration can also be saved to the Grid Control repository in order to standardize across the enterprise:

1. Click on the **Save** button to save the current configuration.

2. Select the option **Save to the EM Repository**.

3. Provide a description such as **GCSOA_<date>_AS_Baseline**.

4. Select the checkbox for saving all the configuration of the application server components, as shown in the following screenshot:

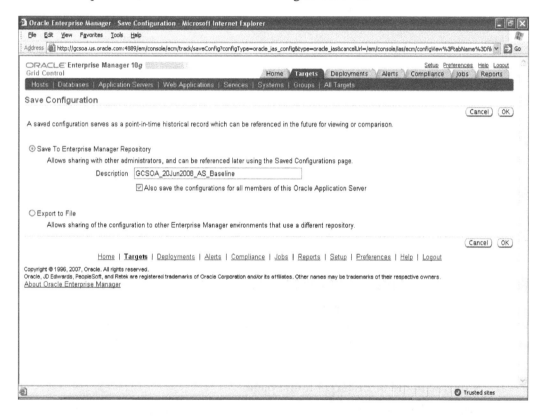

5. Click on **OK** to save the current configuration to the Grid Control repository.

6. Note the confirmation message, and the saved configuration with target name, type, and timestamp.

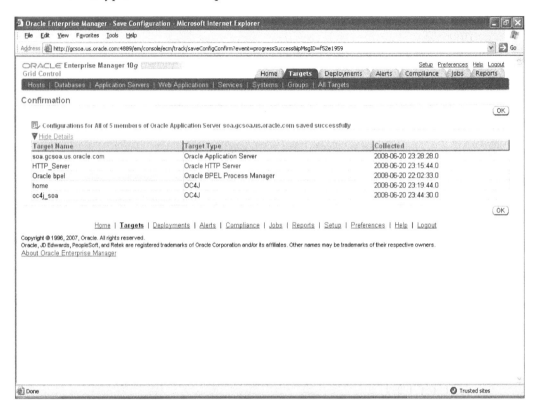

Making changes to the BPEL environment

The Grid Control console is the management interface for one or more BPEL PMs, as well as other target types. For administrative functions such as start/stop, changing configuration properties, and so on, the administrator needs to utilize the product console, in this case BPEL console.

1. Navigate to the BPEL target home page.

2. Under **Related Links**, click on **Adminster (BPEL Console)**.

3. Log in using the **Username** as **oc4jadmin** and **Password** as *welcome1*.

4. Click on the **Manage BPEL Domain** link.

5. This takes you to the admin page for BPEL where you can set domain-level parameters. Select the **Configuration** tab.

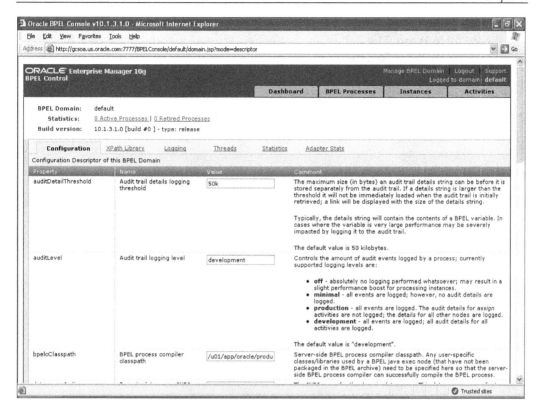

6. Change the following properties:
   - ° **AuditDetailThreshold** to **60k**
   - ° **dspMaxThreads** to **6**
   - ° **dspMinThreads** to **2**
   - ° **LargeDocumentThreshhold** to **60k**

7. Click on the **Apply** button to save the changes.

8. Select the **Logging** tab and select the dropdown to change the logging level for all to **Warn**. The debug level of warn indicates warning messages that are logged to some log, but the application is able to carry on without a problem.

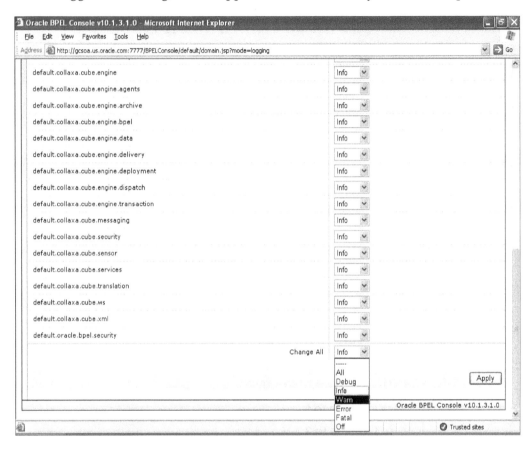

9. Click on **Apply** to save the changes.
10. Select **Logout** to exit the BPEL Control.

Making changes to the Oracle Application Server environment

Similar to the BPEL Console, the application server also comes with its own administrative console to make configuration changes.

1. From the Grid Control home page, click on the **Targets** tab.
2. Select the **Application Servers** sub-tab.

3. Click on the name of the application server — **soademo.gcsoa.us.oracle.com**.

4. This takes you to the home page for the application server.

5. Click on the **Administer** link at the bottom, under the **Related Links** section.

6. Log in to the AS Control console by using the username as **oc4jadmin** and password as *welcome1*.

7. Click on the **oc4j_soa** link to go to the home page for this *oc4j* instance, as shown in the following screenshot:

8. The **oc4j_soa** home page displays key availability and performance metrics for this oc4j instance.

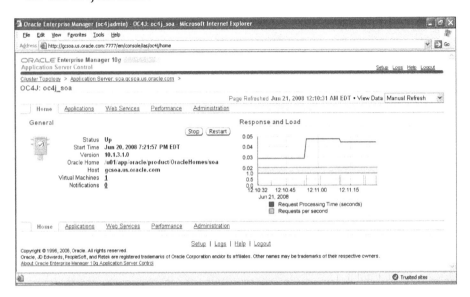

9. Click on the **Administration** tab.

10. Click on the **Go to Task** button next to the **Server Properties** task name, as shown in the following screenshot:

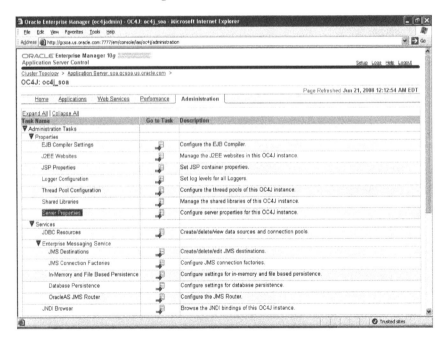

11. Change the **MaxPermSize** value from **126M to 256M**.

12. Click on **Apply** to save the changes. Note the confirmation message.
13. Click on the **Cluster Topology** breadcrumb.
14. Check the box next to the **oc4j_soa**
15. Click on the **Restart** button to restart this oc4j container to make the changes permanent.

16. Click on **Yes** to restart oc4j_soa. Note the confirmation message.

17. Log out of the EM Application Server control after the restart completes. You have now successfully made some changes to the application server properties.

Comparing the current BPEL configuration with a saved baseline

Comparisons are a useful way to detect configuration differences between two or more targets. It is useful to observe the similarities in configuration and, more importantly, the differences in case of a performance problem, or for standardization purposes.

1. Navigate to the BPEL target home page.

2. Click on the **Administration** tab.

3. Click on **Last Collected Configuration**.

4. Click on the **Refresh** button to get the latest configurations updated and wait for sometime.

5. Click on the **Compare** button to start a comparison between the current configuration of the BPEL target and a saved (Production Baseline) configuration.

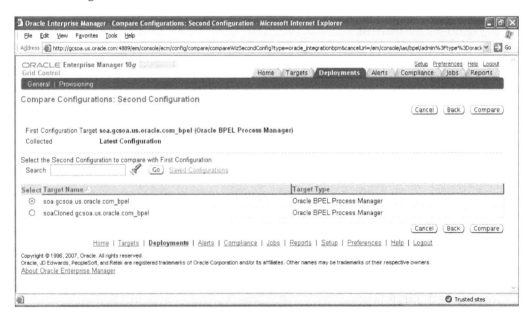

6. Click on the **Saved Configuration** link.

7. Select the **GCSOA_<date>_BPEL_Baseline** for comparison.

8. Click on **Compare** to generate the comparison results.

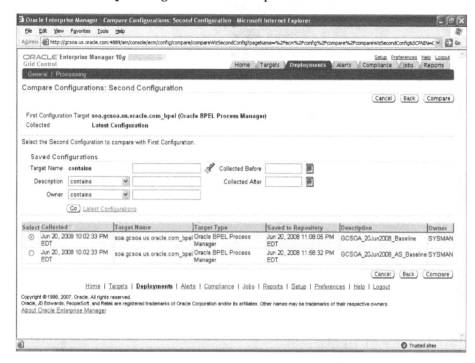

9. View the BPEL target comparison results with a saved baseline.

10. The comparison results between the BPEL targets are presented in four categories. The **Summary** tab lists the status of the four categories.

11. Click on the **Process Manager** tab. The **Process Manager** tab lists the differences or similarities in the general parameters for the targets, including dehydration store and cluster parameters.

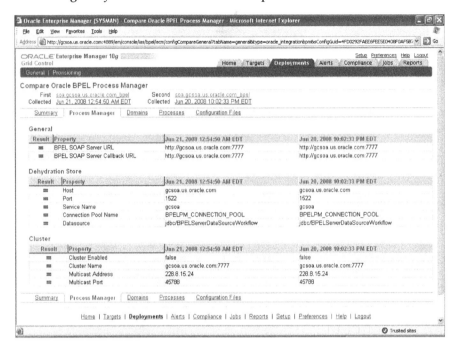

12. Click on the **Domains** tab. The **Domains** tab lists the various domains in the two targets.

13. Click on the *inequality* sign in the **Result** column to view the differences.

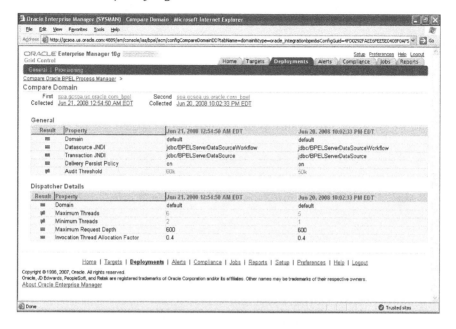

14. Click on the **Compare BPEL Process Manager** breadcrumb.

15. Click on the **Processes** tab. The **Processes** tab compares all the deployed processes. The underlying files within a process are compared.

16. Click on the **Configuration Files** tab, which lists the results of the file comparison.

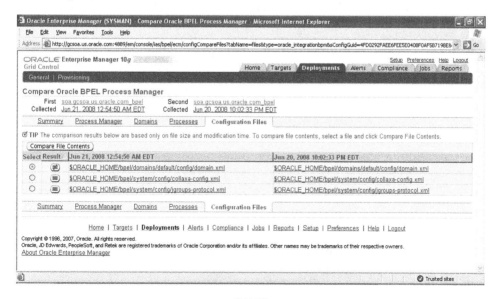

17. Click on the *inequality* sign in the **Result** column to view the differences in file size and modified time.

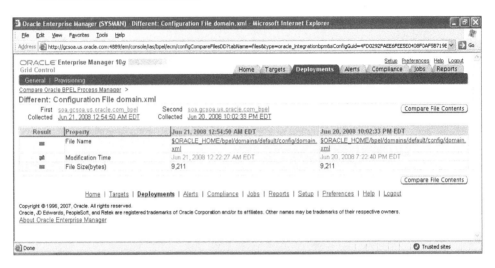

18. Click on the **Back** button of the browser.

19. Click on **Compare File Contents**.

20. View the differences between files on the compare file contents page.

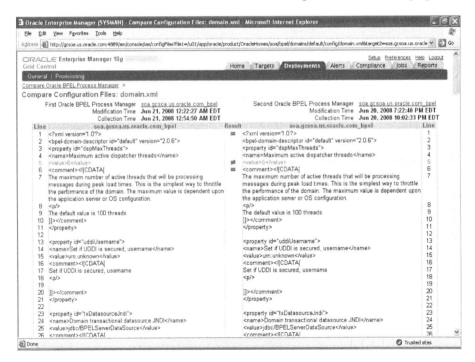

Comparing BPEL process versions for the same process

Grid Control can provide target comparisons for different target types. One of the more interesting comparisons in the BPEL world is to compare successive versions of a BPEL process, or similar BPEL processes on different environments. Grid Control enables the administrator or developer to do just that, thereby assisting with change management and impact analysis.

1. In our current scenario, we will compare two versions of the same BPEL process on the same server.
2. Click the **Compare BPEL Process Manager** breadcrumb.
3. Click on the **Processes** tab.

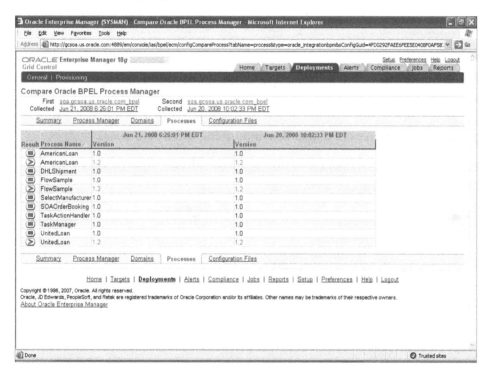

 Notice the differences in the processes across the two targets. You can see that newer versions of the BPEL processes are available for **FlowSample**, **AmericanLoan**, and **UnitedLoan**.

4. Click on the *greater than* sign for the **FlowSample** process.
5. This takes you to the compare process page where you can compare different versions of the process.

6. From the **Version** drop-down list, pick two different versions for the same process.

7. Click on **Compare File Contents**, as shown in the following screenshot:

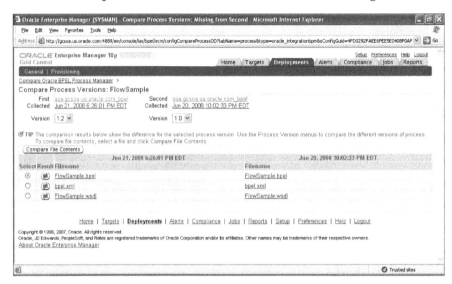

8. Note the differences in the files underlying these processes.

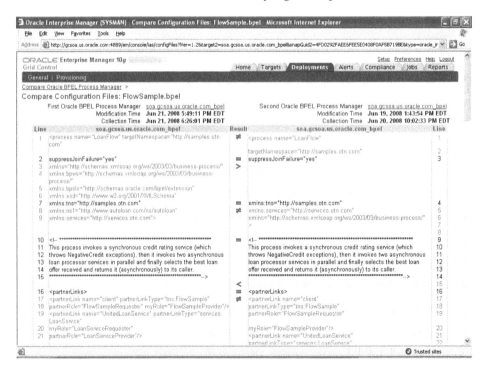

9. By scrolling down, you can see that an additional section has been added to the version 1.2 of the process.

Comparing the current Oracle Application Server configuration with a saved baseline

The same approach can be used for the Oracle application server target as well:

1. Navigate to the home page for the Oracle Application Server target.
2. Select the **Targets** tab and then select the **Application Server** sub-tab.
3. Click on the link for the application server name, such as **soademo.gcsoa.us.oracle.com**, to take you to the application server home page.
4. Click on the **Administration** tab.
5. Click on the **Last collected Configuration**.
6. Click on the **Refresh** button to get the latest configurations updated.
7. Click on the **Compare** button to start a comparison between the current configuration of the application server target and a saved (Production Baseline) configuration.

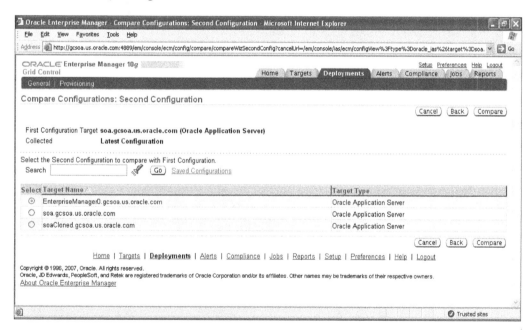

8. Click on the **Saved Configurations** link.
9. Select the **GCSOA_<date>_AS_Baseline** for comparison.

10. Click **Compare** to generate the comparison results.

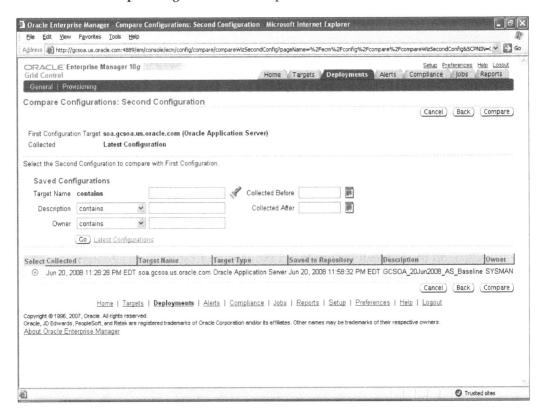

Viewing application server target comparison results with a saved baseline

Once the comparisons have been initiated, the similarities and differences can be observed on the Grid Control user interface:

1. The comparison results between the application server targets are presented in four categories. The **Summary** tab lists the status of the four categories.

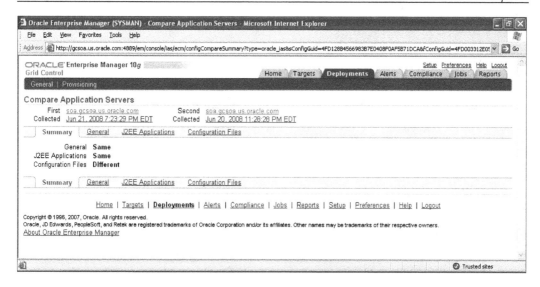

2. Click on the **General** tab to view key parameters values and changes from the baseline.

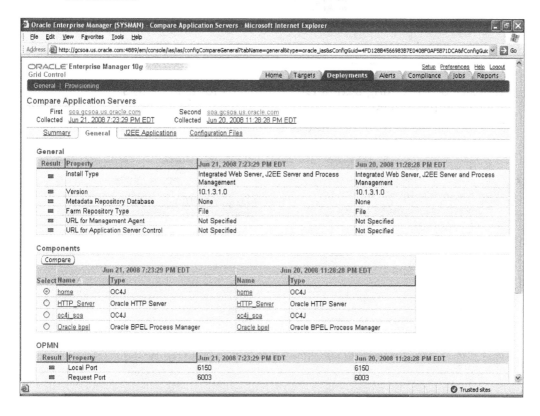

3.   Click on the **J2EE Applications** tab to look for any changes.

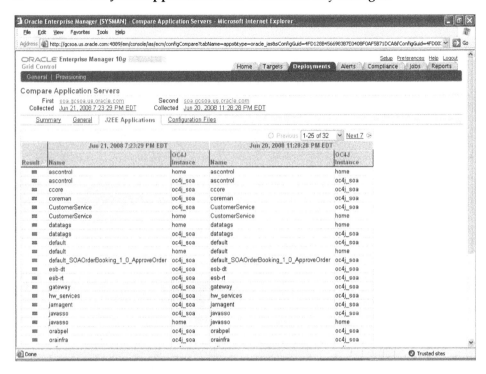

4.   Click on the **Configuration Files** tab to look for key changes to the configuration files.

5.   Click on the radio button next to the *inequality* sign displayed.

6. Click on **Compare File Contents** to view the actual changes from the baseline version.

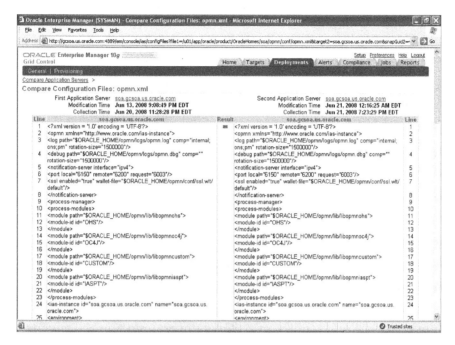

7. Observe changes to the **MaxPermSize**.

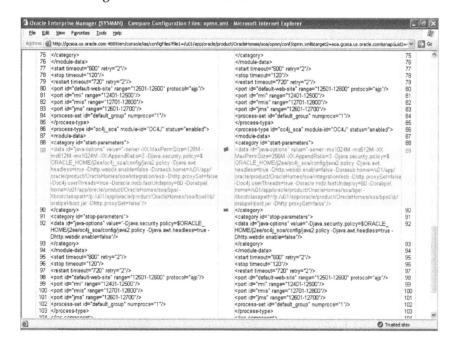

Summary

Configuration management is critical for administrators to control change within the environment and troubleshoot problems associated with changing configurations. With Grid Control's configuration management capabilities, administrators can manage change and reduce time to troubleshoot problems.

In this chapter, we discussed configuration management and how it applies to BPEL PM and the application server target. We discussed the configuration overview for both target types, looked at the most recent configuration information, and saved a reference "gold" configuration snapshot to the Grid Control repository. Then we proceeded to make a few configuration changes via the individual product consoles. It was fairly simple to observe these changes in Grid Control, as well as compare the changes with the "gold" standard. Further, it was also useful to compare BPEL process versions and note the changes across successive versions.

Configuration management has been extended with Enterprise Manager's acquisition of two new products, namely **Configuration Change Console** (**CCC**) and **Application Change Console** (**ACC**). With these two products, administrators can view changes actively as they happen, as well as roll back and roll forward to a desired configuration.

The next few chapters will walkthrough SOA suite provisioning and cloning.

9
SOA Suite Cloning

Software maintenance often accounts for 70 percent of overall cost and that includes licensing. Enterprises have to worry about maintaining their software, which includes product updates, security updates, hardware updates, and environment refreshes. These are time-consuming tasks that require human expertise in several areas. As the software ages, an enterprise still needs to maintain this human expertise for legacy software that, while critical to the business, can be expensive and sometimes negate the overall business value by increasing the cost of ownership.

More and more enterprises are turning to automated lifecycle management tools to help with this heavy lifting related to software lifecycle maintenance. It is important to have the right strategy in place to plan for maintenance. Maintenance should be part of the overall strategy, not an afterthought.

This chapter covers:

- Challenges
- Solution
- Step-by-step exercises:
    - Adding an Oracle Application Server Cluster to Grid Control
    - Stopping application server processes
    - Creating a component in the Grid Control Software Library
    - Cloning an Oracle Application Server and SOA applications
    - Validating a newly created cluster

Challenges

In today's data centers, services often need to be provisioned in short order. These services could consist of complex multitier configurations, such as Oracle Application Server and SOA application software. An administrator has to go through multiple steps to clone an SOA Suite from one installation to another. The steps include cloning copied files, configuring them, and making changes to reflect the new installation. Several Oracle administrators have database cloning skills, but most do not possess the expertise to clone Application Server, let alone the SOA Suite. Manual installations of such services are often time consuming and error prone.

Solution

Grid Control provides a flexible and scalable way to clone tested images to multiple hosts. Specifically, Grid Control offers a predefined, fully customizable procedure for cloning Oracle Application Server and SOA applications. The procedure enables administrators to either create a new Oracle Application Server instance or Oracle Application Sever Cluster based on an existing, reference application server or cluster; thereby automating common IT tasks such as creating a production SOA Suite environment based on a test or stage, or such as extending an existing Oracle Application Server Cluster to accommodate an increase in load.

Step-by-step exercises

This set of step-by-step exercises will walkthrough cloning an Oracle SOA Suite 10.1.3.x deployed on Oracle Application Server 10.1.3.x.

Adding an Oracle Application Server Cluster to Grid Control

The first step is to create the application server cluster target in order to clone it later.

 In order to create a new cluster via cloning, Grid Control must be aware of an existing, installed cluster from which to clone.

1. From the Grid Control home page, click on the **Targets | Middleware** tab.

 In the table, you should see a minimum of two Oracle Application Server targets: one hosting the Grid Control application and the other hosting the SOA Suite, as discussed in previous chapters. While the Oracle Application Server instance hosting the SOA Suite has been discovered in Enterprise Manager, the cluster in which it is a member has not yet been discovered.

2. From the **Add** drop-down menu, select **Oracle Application Server Cluster** and click on **Go**, as shown in the following screenshot:

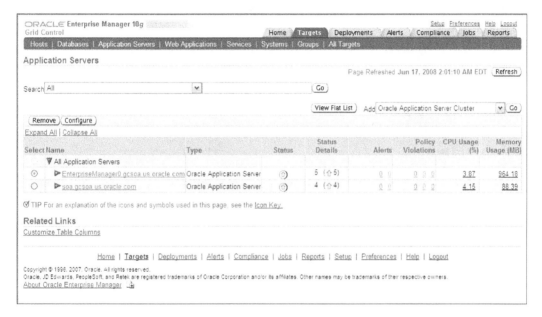

3. A page appears prompting for information on the existing cluster. Provide a name for the cluster, such as **Cluster 10131**.

4. To specify an application server instance that is a member of the cluster, click on the *flashlight* icon.

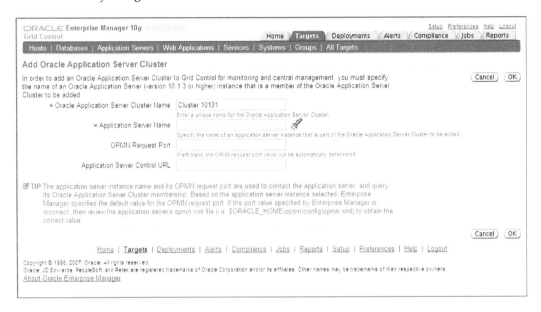

5. On the **Search and Select: Targets** page, select the name of an application server instance that is a member of the cluster and click on the **Select** button, as shown in the following screenshot:

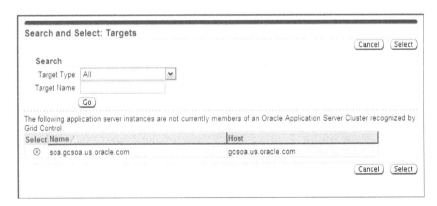

6. The remaining fields on the **Add Oracle Application Server Cluster** page are automatically populated based on your selection, as shown in the next screenshot. Click on **OK**.

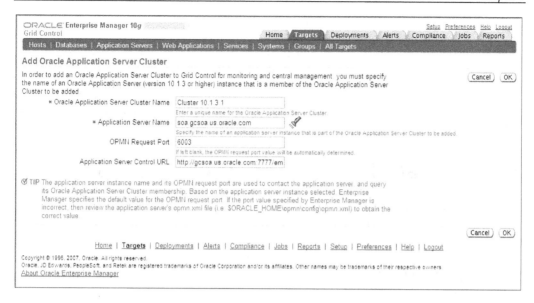

7. A confirmation message appears at the top of the screen to confirm that the cluster was successfully added to Enterprise Manager, and **Cluster 10.1.3.1** appears as a new target in the table with the **soa.gcsoa.us.oracle. com** application server shown as a member of that cluster, as shown in the following screenshot:

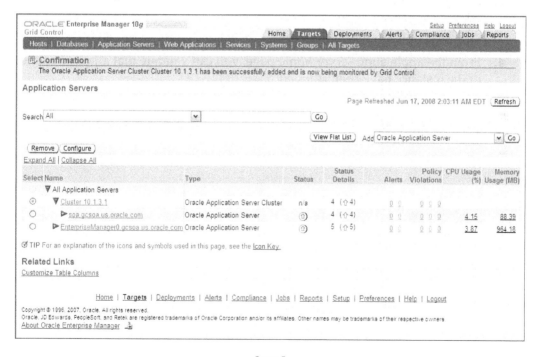

Now that an Oracle Application Server Cluster has been added to Grid Control, you can use the cluster as a reference or source for performing a wide range of operations. For the purpose of this exercise, we will use the discovered cluster to create a "gold image" component in the Grid Control Software Library, and then use the gold image component in the library to create a new Oracle Application Server Cluster target.

Stopping application server processes

Stopping the application server processes is recommended in order to take a copy of the data and the configuration.

Prior to creating a gold image component or creating a new cluster via cloning, you should first stop the existing, installed application server processes already running on the machine.

To stop the Oracle Application Server processes, follow these steps:

1. Log in as the application server owner on the Linux or Windows machine (for example, oracle).

2. Navigate to the bin directory, that is,
   `cd/u01/app/oracle/product/OracleHomes/soa/opmn/bin`.

3. Stop the application server processes by using: `./opmnctl stopall`.

4. From the application server home page, you can validate that all components of the instance have been stopped.

If the application server instance status continues to read **Up**, click on the **Refresh** icon on the page.

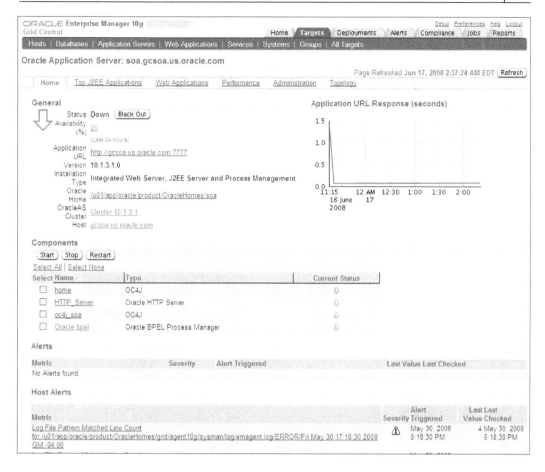

Creating a component in the Grid Control Software Library

Grid Control allows you to clone Oracle Application Server software directly from an existing install base, or from a component stored in the Software Library. In this exercise, we will clone from a component stored in the Software Library.

> Prior to creating components in the Software Library, you must first configure the Software Library. For information on how to configure the Software Library outside of exercise, refer to section *18.7 Setting Up and Configuring a Software Library with Oracle Enterprise Manager* in the *Oracle Enterprise Manager Advanced Configuration 10g Release 4* guide posted on the Oracle Technology Network.

1. Navigate to the **Deployments** tab and click on the **Provisioning** sub-tab.

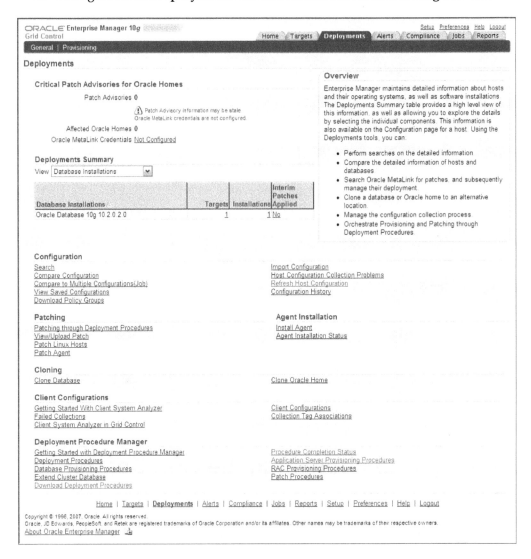

2. On the **Components** property page, click on the **Create Component** button located directly above the table on the far right-hand side, shown in the following screenshot:

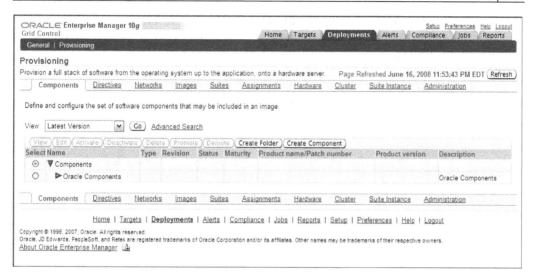

3. The **Create Component** wizard appears with the **Describe** page displayed. Ensure that the component selected in the **Type** drop-down menu is **Oracle iAS Clone**, and supply a name for the component to be created, such as **SOA 10.1.3.1 Gold Image**. The remaining fields are optional. Click on **Next**, as shown in the following screenshot:

4. The **Configure** page of the **Create Component** wizard appears. Click on the *flashlight* icon to select a host name on which the existing software has been installed.

5. From the **Select Clone Source** page, select the host on which the Oracle Application Server SOA Suite 10.1.3.1.0 product has been installed. This will be the source Oracle home that will be zipped up, compressed, and stored in the Software Library. It will be used later in the hands-on lab as the gold, reference image from which to clone. Click on **OK**.

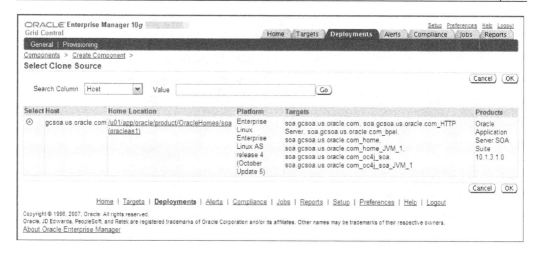

6. Provide the following information on the **Configure** page of the wizard:

   Username: **oracle**

   Password: *welcome1*

   Working Directory: **/tmp**

7. Leave the **Internet Directory Username** and **Internet Directory Password** fields blank, unless you are using an Oracle Internet Directory. Click on **Next**, as shown in the following screenshot:

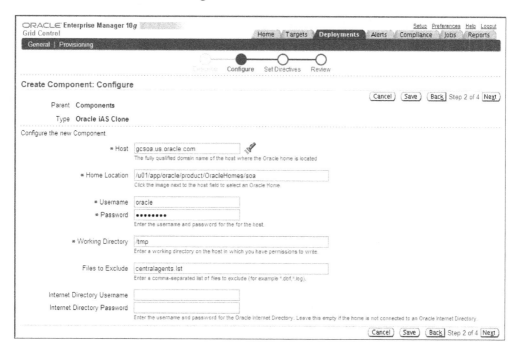

8. No inputs or edits are required on the **Set Directives** page of the **Create Component** wizard. Click on **Next**, shown in the following screenshot:

9. Review the content on the **Review** page of the wizard to ensure the inputted data is accurate. Click on **Finish**, as shown in the next screenshot:

10. A confirmation message will appear at the top of the page indicating that a job was submitted to create the Oracle Application Server 10.1.3.1 SOA Suite component in the Grid Control Software Library. To track progress of the job, click on the link identifying the job execution ID in the confirmation message.

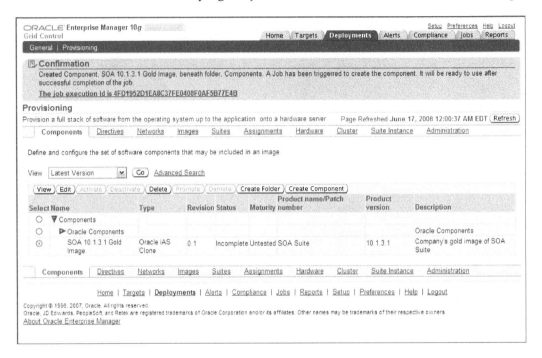

11. The **Summary** wizard of the **Job Run** page appears. Ensure that the job completes successfully. This might take several minutes to complete, depending on the nature of the Oracle Application Server configuration.

12. Use the web browser's **Refresh** button to refresh the job's status until you see that the job status has changed from **Running** to **Succeeded**.

13. Return to the **Provisioning** sub-tab under the **Deployments** tab to see the newly created component in the Software Library table. In order to use the component during a clone operation, you must activate the component. Select the newly created Oracle Application Server 10.1.3.1 SOA Suite component in the table and click on the **Activate** button along the top of the table.

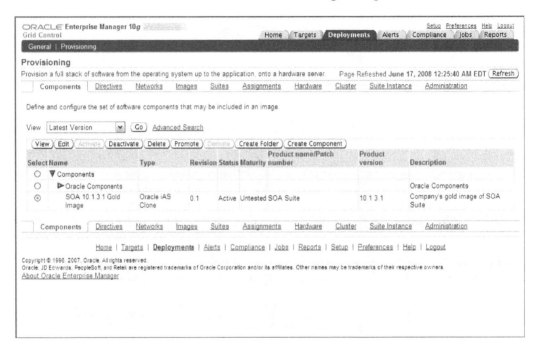

 An active, gold image component for the existing cluster is now in the Software Library and, as such can be used as the source image from which to create a new application server instance and cluster.

Cloning Oracle Application Server and SOA applications

Now we are ready to clone the Oracle Application Server with the underlying SOA applications, using the out-of-box deployment procedures:

1. Navigate to the **General** sub-tab from under the **Deployments** tab. Click on the **Application Server Provisioning Procedures** link in the **Deployment Procedure Manager** section at the bottom of the page.

2. A list of out-of-the-box application server-related deployment procedures appears. Select the procedure named **Application Server Deployment 10.1.3.1SOA** and click on **Schedule Deployment**.

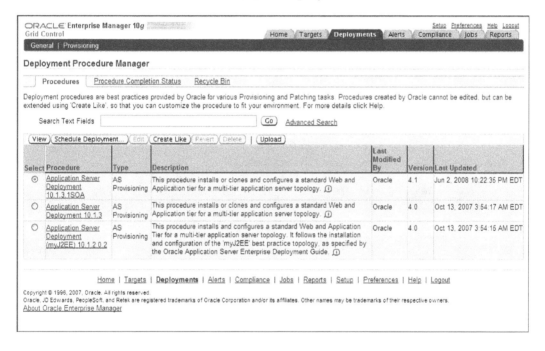

3. A multi-step wizard appears to guide you through scheduling the cloning operation. As stated earlier, when you clone Oracle Application Server, you have the choice to clone from a source that is already installed and discovered in the Enterprise Manager environment or to clone from a source that is stored in the Software Library. Because we created a gold image component in the Software Library earlier in the exercise, select the **Select from Software Library** option. Because the only component that we created in the Software Library was the Application Tier, we will only clone the Application Tier from the Software Library in this hands-on lab. Click on the *flashlight* icon associated with the **Source for App Tier** section.

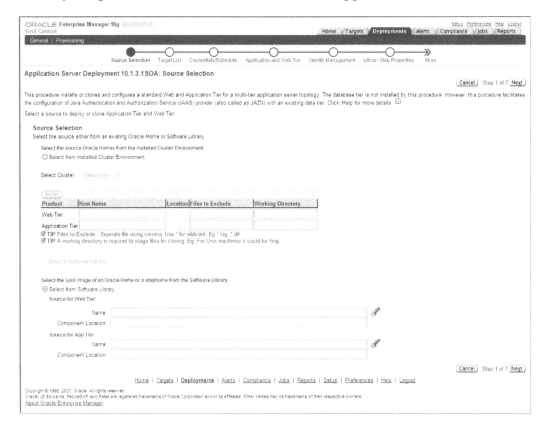

4. From the **Select Component for Application Tier** page, select the **Component Name** as the one that we created earlier (the recommended name is **SOA 10.1.3.1 Gold Image**) and click on the **Select** button, as shown in the following screenshot:

5. You are then returned to the **Source Selection** page of the wizard with the details for the **Source for App Tier** automatically populated for you. Click on **Next**, as shown in the following screenshot:

6. On the **Target List** page of the wizard, click on the **Add** button, as seen on the following screenshot:

7. On the **Select Target(s) for Application Tier** page, select the **Host Name** (for example, **gcsoa.us.oracle.com**) as the destination machine to clone the cluster to. Click on the **Select** button, as seen in the next screenshot:

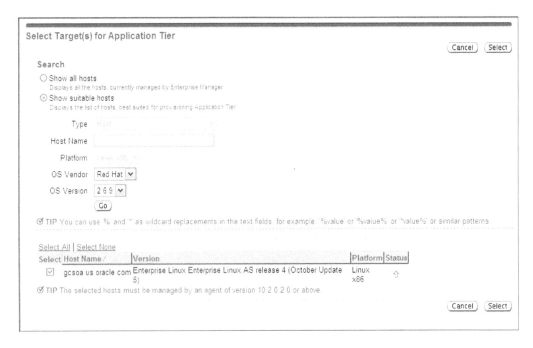

8. You are then returned to the **Target List** page of the wizard with the details for the **Application Tier Hosts** automatically populated for you. Click on **Next**, as shown in the following screenshot:

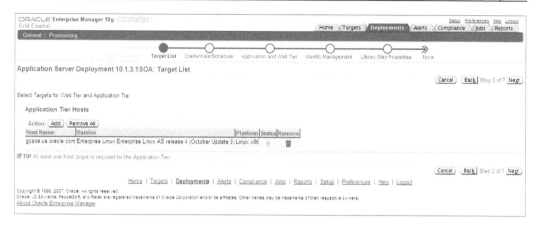

9. On the **Credentials/Schedule** page of the wizard, specify the following information concerning the host credentials for the destination machine:

   Host Credentials: Same for all Oracle Homes

   Username: oracle

   Password: *welcome1*

10. Because the deployment procedure leverages the Enterprise Manager Job System, you can schedule the cloning operation immediately or at a future date and time. For the purposes of this exercise, keep the default selection as **One Time (Immediately)**, as seen in the next screenshot. Click on **Next**.

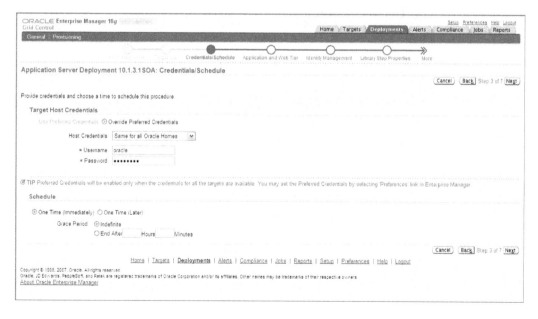

11. On the **Application and Web Tier** page of the wizard, specify the following information, as shown in the next screenshot:

   ◦ **Cluster Details** section:

   - **Cluster Name: myJ2EECluster**
   - **App Tier Install Base Directory** : **/u01/app/oracle/product/ OracleHomes/soa_clone**
   - **Multicast Address: 227.0.0.1**
   - **Multicast Port: 6789**

 In this exercise, the source and destination Oracle homes are on the same machine. However, you need to ensure that the Application Tier Install Base Directory you specify is unique. The existing installation's directory /u01/app/oracle/product/OracleHomes/soa is specified as the default value. So you must change the default value to make it unique.

   ◦ **Instance Details** section:

   - **Application Tier Instance Name: soaCloned**
   - **Source OC4J Admin Password: welcome1**
   - **OC4J Admin Password**: *welcome1*
   - **Confirm OC4J Admin Password**: *welcome1*

   ◦ **Port Details** section:

   Port: 8888

   ◦ In the **Additional Parameters** section, leave the **Application Tier** field blank.

   ◦ In the **Identity Management Configuration** section, select the **None** option.

12. Click on **Next**.

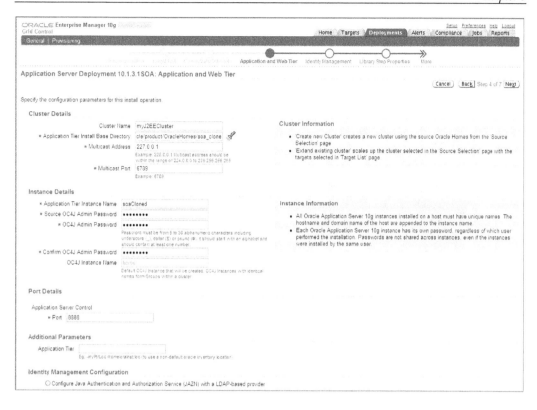

13. On the **Library Step Properties** page of the wizard, provide the following
    information concerning the dehydration store to be affiliated with the new
    cloned application server instance:

    ○ **Database Vendor**: oracle

    ○ **Database User Name**: sys

    ○ **Database Password**: *<Enter your database system password>*

    ○ **Database Hostname and Port**: gcsoa.us.oracle.com:1522

    ○ **Service Name**: gcsoa

To successfully clone, specifying "sys" as the database username is not required. However, the database username provided must have been granted the DBA role. This user is leveraged to ensure that the database is valid (can connect to it, correct version, correct edition, and that the relevant SOA-related schemas exist).

14. Click on **Next**.

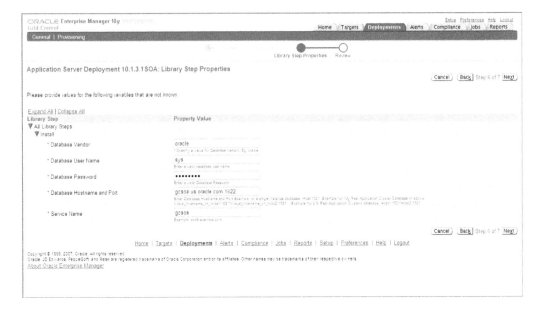

15. Review the content displayed on the **Review** page of the wizard to ensure inputs were supplied properly. Click on **Finish**.

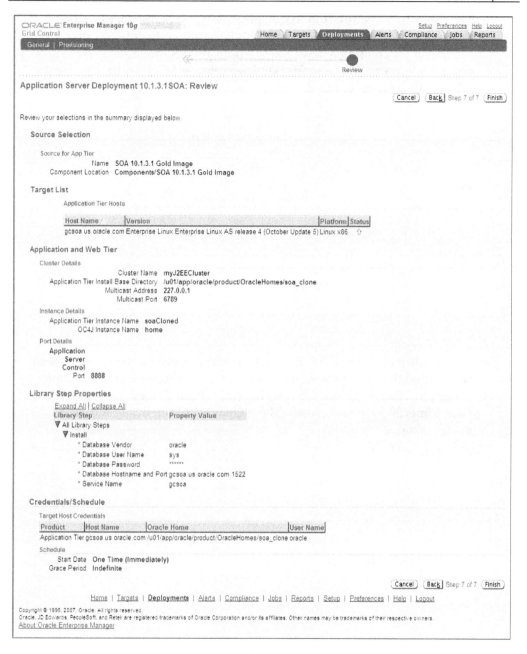

16. The **Procedure Completion Status** property page on the **Deployment Procedure Manager** page appears. This shows you the Job Run that was just submitted for creating a new Oracle Application Server based on the gold image component stored in the Software Library. Click on the link for the Job Run that was submitted.

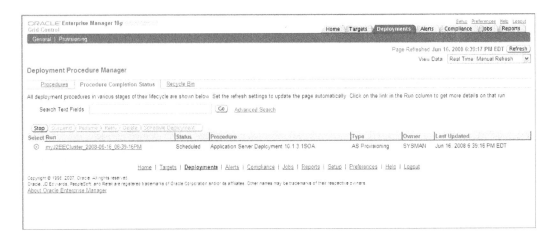

17. The **Status** page for this Job Run will appear displaying the status of each step within the deployment procedure. To track progress of the cloning operation, change the refresh interval in the **View Data** drop-down list to **Real Time: 30 Second Refresh**. The page will automatically refresh with the updated status.

18. When the **Status** refreshes to **Succeeded**, the clone operation has finished. In this exercise, this takes about 21 minutes.

Validating a newly created cluster

After the deployment procedure completes, we need to validate the newly created application server instance. For the purpose of this exercise, we will verify that the new Oracle Application Server target appears in Enterprise Manager and then login to the BPEL Console:

1. Navigate to the **Targets | Middleware** sub-tab.

2. The newly created Oracle Application Server target named **soaCloned.gcsoa. us.oracle.com** appears in the table. Click on that name, as shown in the following screenshot:

3. The Oracle Application Server home page for the new instance appears. Ensure that identical components (that is, **home, HTTP_Server, oc4j_soa, Oracle bpel**) appear in the **Components** table as existed for the source Oracle Application Server target. Click on the **Oracle bpel** component, as seen in the next sceenshot:

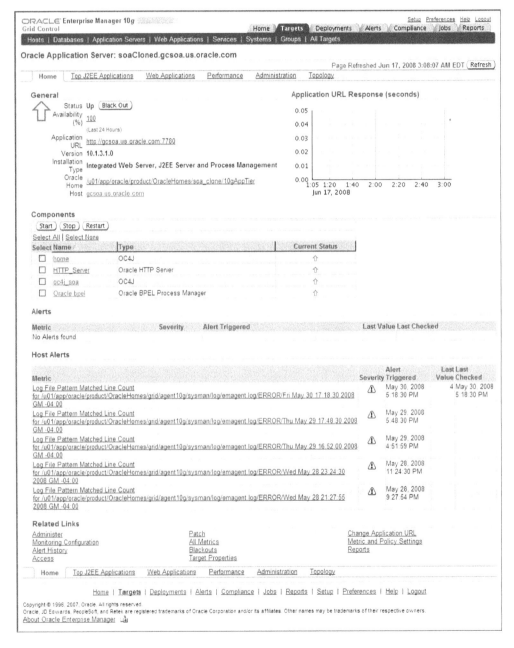

4. The **Oracle BPEL Process Manager** home page appears. In the **Related Links** section at the bottom of the page, click on **Administer (BPEL Console)**, as seen in the following screenshot:

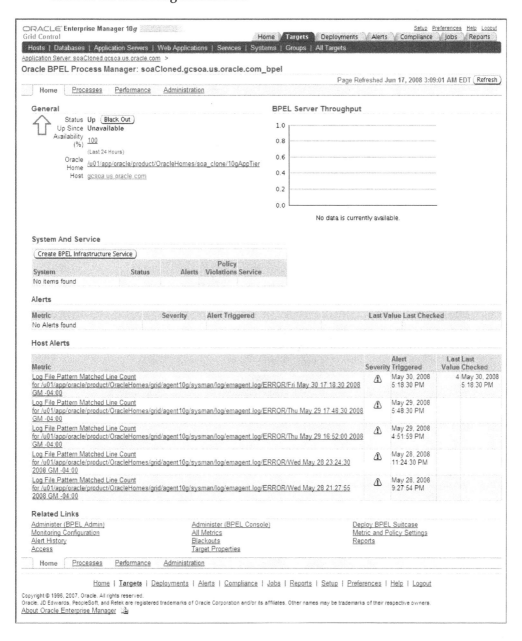

5. On the BPEL console login page, provide the following information:

Username: oc4jadmin

Password: *welcome1*

6. The BPEL Control console appears, and on the page several **Deployed BPEL Processes** are listed. Ensure that these processes on the target server are the same as the ones on the source server.

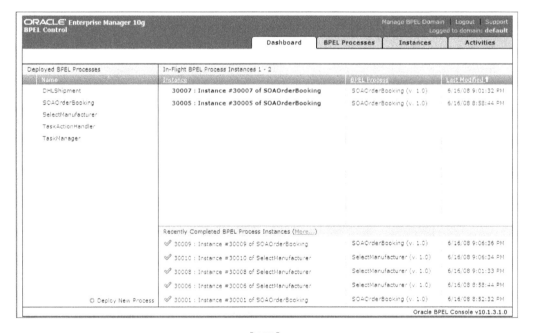

Summary

Managing the lifecycle of software and services is a time-consuming and error-prone task. Administrators can spend several days and weeks planning and implementing provisioning and patching tasks. Grid Control greatly simplifies these complex tasks so that administrators can focus on more strategic areas, and the enterprise can be more agile in managing the lifecycle of software and services.

In this chapter, we discussed the steps to clone Oracle Application Server and SOA Suite. Specifically, we discussed adding an Oracle Application Server cluster to Grid Control, stopping application server processes, making a copy of the application server and storing it in the Grid Control Software Library, cloning the application server and SOA Suite, and finally validating the newly created cluster. It's important to note that Grid Control copies the data and the configurations from the source to the target cluster. The provisioning and cloning solutions are complemented by patching solutions. New features include similar coverage for the SOA Suite on Oracle WebLogic server, post the BEA acquisition, which provides administrators relief in managing SOA deployments on WebLogic server.

10
Web Application Monitoring

Measuring and managing end users' performance has become increasingly important to ensure customer satisfaction. While services and infrastructure might be healthy and available within the data centre's firewalls, consumers may still have problems accessing services externally via the Internet. This then becomes a guessing game to isolate the problem to the customer's Internet Service Provider, or to the provider's faulty service. Further, in the age of Twitter and Facebook, providers are increasingly at risk with distributed denial-of-service-type attacks. A lot of providers today, such as Amazon, Google, and Salesforce.com, provide publicly available information about the current and historical status of their services.

Increasingly, service-level agreements are tied to the end user's experience of interacting with a service. If the end users cannot access a service, then a simple "tweet" on Twitter can lead to a rapid chain reaction of user complaints that may quickly become a source of negative publicity for the provider. In today's world, provider's have no place to hide when consumers are faced with unavailable or poorly performing services. In some cases, this may lead to money-back requests based on contractual obligations.

This chapter talks about:

- Challenges
- Solution
- Step-by-step exercises:
    - ° Creating a web application
    - ° Recording a web transaction as a Service Test
    - ° Adding Beacons to run the Service Test
    - ° Adding performance and usage metrics
    - ° Viewing web transaction playback

Challenges

A web application administrator wants to have better visibility into the availability or performance as seen by end users. The administrator wants to closely watch a list of critical URLs that are "always expected to be alive and responsive" or monitor the performance of web applications from various regions, domains, or of a specific set of visitors, to ensure that the consumers are receiving optimal performance. The ability to understand the impact of the performance problems is critical. It is also useful to learn about the pages, visitors, domains, and regions impacted by performance problems.

Solution

Grid Control comes with a transaction-recording capability that lets you record web transactions that emulates end users. Grid Control tracks all response times of all URLs for all visitors that have accessed your application. Grid Control can not only emulate web traffic, but also emulates tnsping, IMAP, SQL, and several other protocols. By monitoring the number of hits combined with performance metrics, and analyzing the response times by URL, domain, region, visitor, and web server, you can clearly assess the impact of performance degradation problems on your user base. Further drilldowns provide you with Web server response time and load distribution information to help you efficiently balance server resources.

Step-by-step exercises

This set of step-by-step exercises will walkthrough managing web applications.

Creating a web application

A web application is a specific target type in Grid Control used to monitor one or more URLs for availability, performance, and SLA reporting.

 Please perform this exercise only on Internet Explorer. You need to be connected to the Internet for this exercise to download Microsoft libraries for the web transaction recorder.

1. From the Grid Control home page, click on the **Targets | Web Applications** tab.

2. Click on the **Add** button to add a new web application, as seen in the next screenshot.

 Web application is a special service in Grid Control. There are other service types such as generic service, aggregate service, and so on.

3. On the **General** step, as shown in the following screenshot:
   ○ Enter the web application name as **SOA Order Booking Client**.
   ○ Select **Time Zone** as **Use System Time Zone**.
   ○ **Enter the Homepage URL** as `http://gcsoa.us.oracle.com:7777/soademo`.

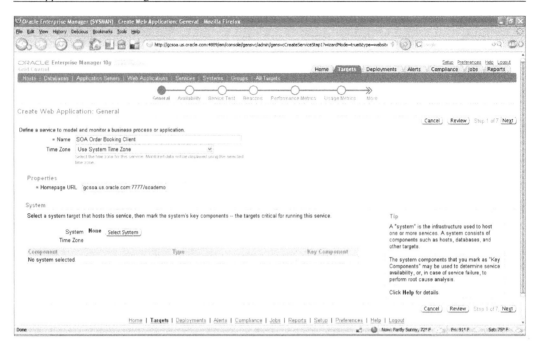

- ° Click on **Select System**.
- ° Select the radio button for **soa_infra_system** in the pop-up window.
- ° Click on **Select**, as shown in the next screenshot:

 A System is a collection of targets in Grid Control. A System has to be created from the **Systems** tab, before a web application (or other service) can be based on that System.

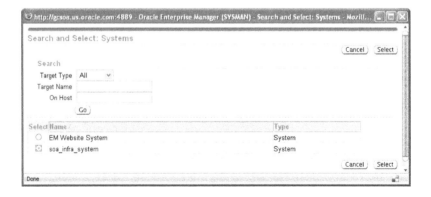

- ° Review the key components for the System. You can uncheck certain components on which the **SOA Order Booking Client** does not depend.

- ° Click on **Next**, as shown in the following screenshot:

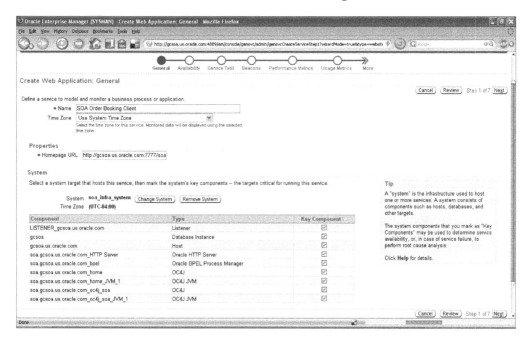

4. On the **Availability** step:

- ° Select to define availability based on **Service Test**.

- ° Click on **Next**, as shown in the next screenshot:

 Availability can be defined based on Service Test or System. Further, availability can be defined based on up/down status as well as usage metrics. Service Test-based availability can be defined as the status of one or more recorded web transactions as tested by one or more agents (Beacons). System-based availability is determined on the status of the underlying system components—either all or one component can be up based on the requirement.

Recording a web transaction as a Service Test

Once the web application target type has been created, we can start to record
end-user-type web transactions using an inbuilt recorder:

1. On the **Service Test** step, fill in the following fields as shown in the
    next screenshot:

    ° Select a Service Test name as **Order Submission Test**.

    ° Select the radio button for **Record a transaction**.

    ° Click on **Go**.

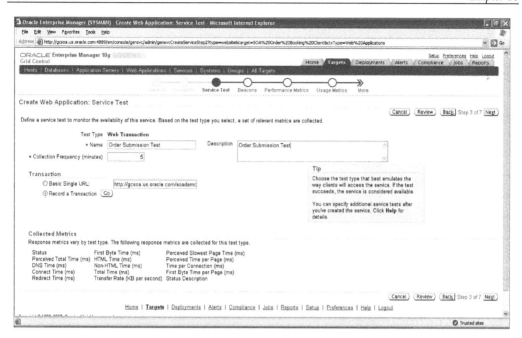

- ° A recorder will be downloaded. Please click on **Install**.

 If the Active X settings are set to high security, download will not happen. To change ActiveX-related settings in Internet Explorer, go to **Tools** | **Internet Options** | **Security** | **Custom level...** and find and change all **ActiveX**-related settings to **Enable** or **Prompt**.

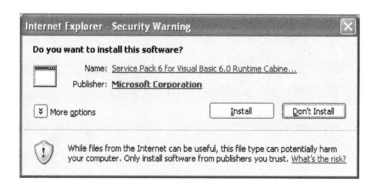

°   After the installation, you will be taken to the recording main page.

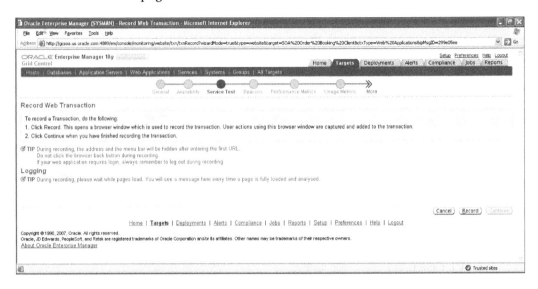

2. Click on the **Record** button to start recording a transaction. This opens a browser window, which is used to record the transaction. User actions using this browser window are captured and added to the transaction.

3. Enter the URL as `http://gcsoa.us.oracle.com:7777/soademo` in the browser window.

4. Enter the **Email** as **sking@soademo.org** and **Password** as *welcome1*, and click on **Login**, as shown in the following screenshot:

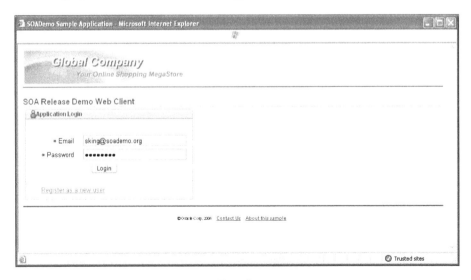

5. On successful login, you will see the screen in the following screenshot:

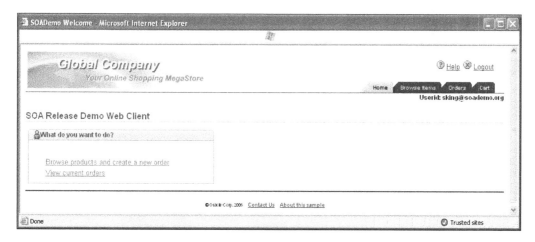

6. Click on **Browse products and create a new order** and then click the radio button for **Playstation2**. Click on **View Details**.

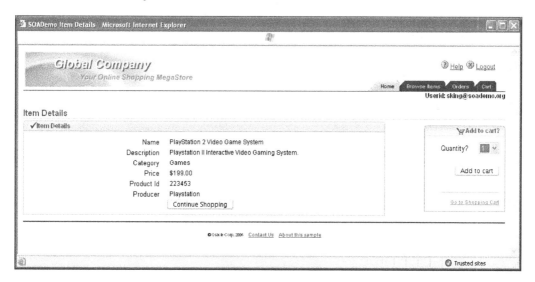

7. Select **Quantity** as **1** and click on the **Add to Cart**, as shown in the following screenshot:

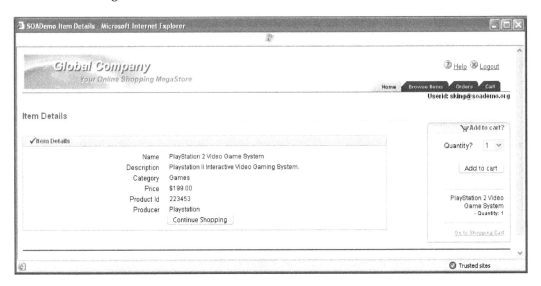

8. Click on **Go To Shopping Cart**.

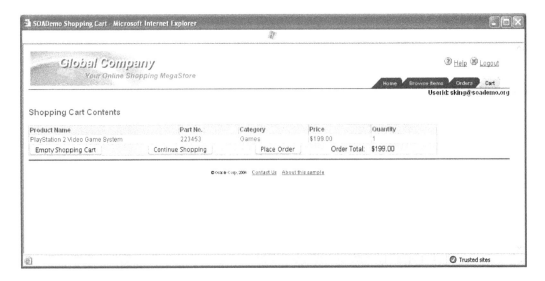

9. Click on the **Place Order** button. Click on the **Orders** tab to view orders submitted. Click on the **logout** link and after going back to the login page, close the browser window.

10. On the **Record Web Transaction** page, click on **Continue**, as you have completed the recording of the transaction, as seen in the following screenshot:

11. You will be taken to the **Success Strings Suggestion** page.

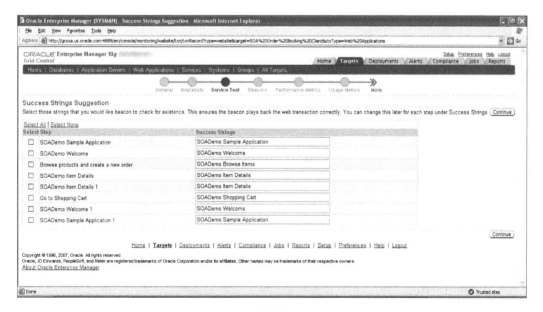

Adding Beacons to run the Service Test

Once the web transactions have been created, we need to set up the agents or Beacons to fire these transactions so that Grid Control can record and report on the transaction metrics:

1. Click on **Continue** to review the Service Test.

2. Click on **Continue** once again.

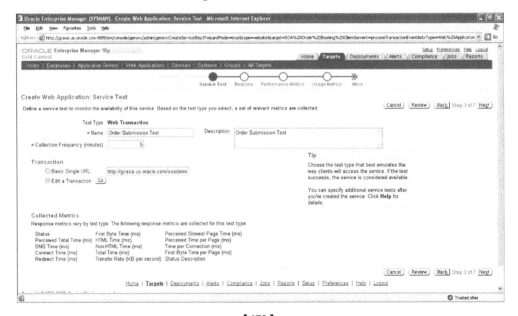

3. Click on **Next** to now select the Beacon.

 Beacons are Grid Control agents configured to emulate end-user behavior by running recorded Service Tests. Frequently, these are deployed outside the firewall to test applications from an end-user perspective. Beacons are deployed where users are located, typically one per geographical segment. Beacons help to break down the end-user time into network time and server time, which helps to isolate user-related problems.

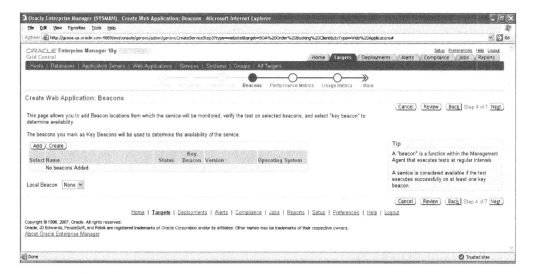

4. Click on **Add** and then select the Beacon, as shown in the following screenshot:

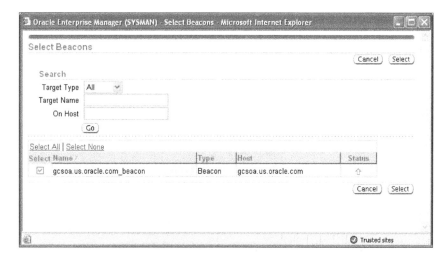

5. Click on **Select**.

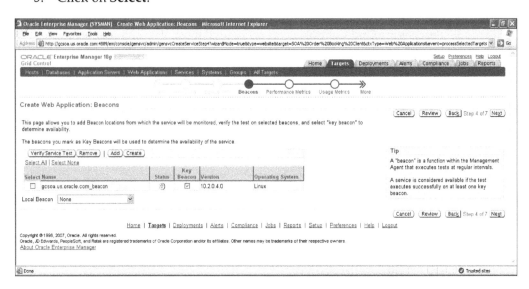

Adding performance and usage metrics

As Grid Control collects several metrics for a web transaction, you can specify specific metrics to be included in the performance and usage buckets:

1. Continuing from the previous step, click on **Next** to now define **Performance Metrics**.

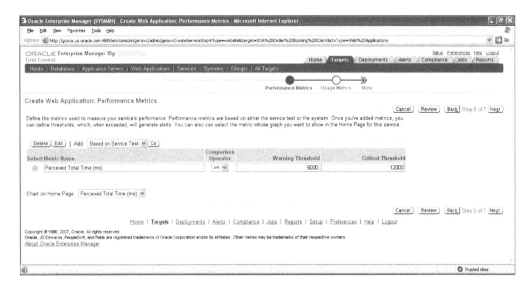

2. Select **Add** as **Based on Service Test** and click on **Go**.

3. Select **Metric** as **Transfer Rate (KB per second)** and click on **Continue**, as shown in the following screenshot:

4. Enter a **Warning Threshold** of **6000** and a **Critical Threshold** of **12000**. You can add additional metrics similarly. Then click on **Next**, as shown in the following screenshot:

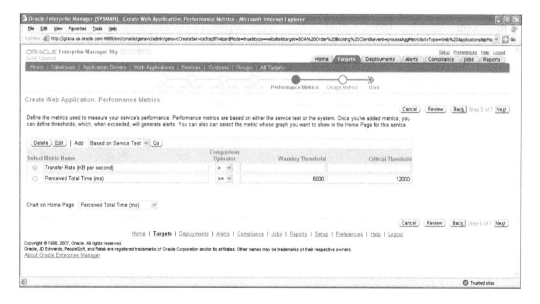

5. You will now be taken to the **Usage Metrics** screen, as seen in the next screenshot. Usage metrics measure user demand for your service. You can define usage metrics based on the metrics of one or more system components. Once you've added metrics, you can define thresholds, which, when exceeded, will generate alerts. You can also select the metric whose graph you want to show in the home page for this service.

6. You can select from a number of target types. For each target type, you can select from a large number of available metrics.

7. For example let's select **Target Type** as **Oracle HTTP Server** and select the metric **Percentage of Requests that Were Failures**

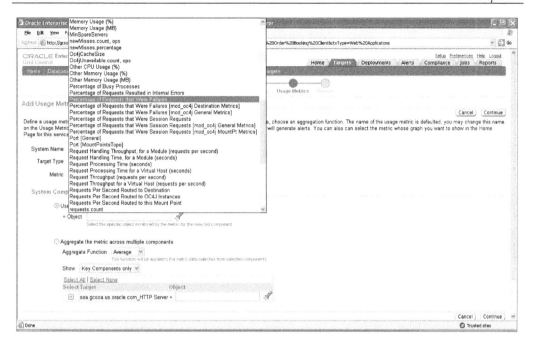

8. Click on the *flashlight* for the object and then select **Mount Point** as **/soademo**.

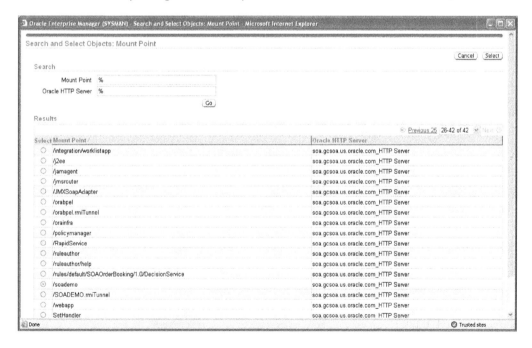

9. On clicking **Select**, you will see the page shown in the following screenshot:

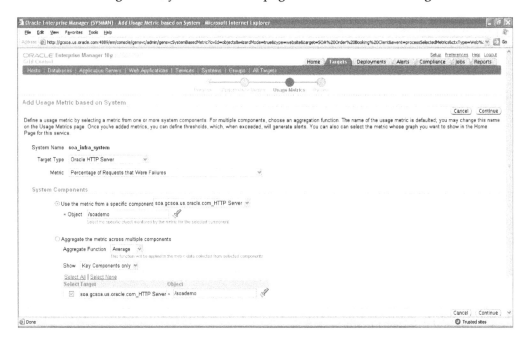

10. Click on **Continue** and then provide a **Warning Threshold** of **10** and a **Critical Threshold** of **20**.

11. Click on **Next** to review all the selections made so far and then click on **Finish**.

12. You have now successfully added the web application with the appropriate recorded service tests, as well as performance and usage metrics.

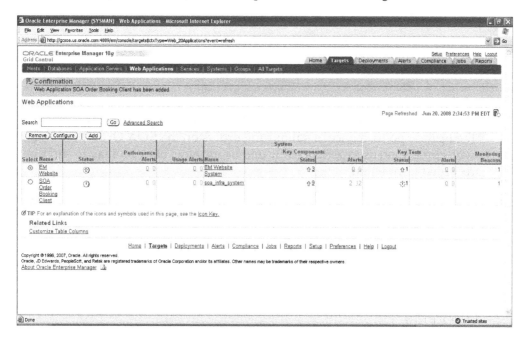

Viewing web transaction playback

After recording the transaction, it is useful to view what has been recorded for verification.

1. To view the recorded Service Test transaction, click on **Targets**, then on the **Web Applications** tab.

2. Click on the **SOA OrderBooking Client** application.

3. In the **Key Test Summary** section, click on **Order Submission Test**. Observe the historic performance of submitting orders on the **SOA OrderBooking** web application as experienced by end users. Now click on **Play** to run the recorded transaction.

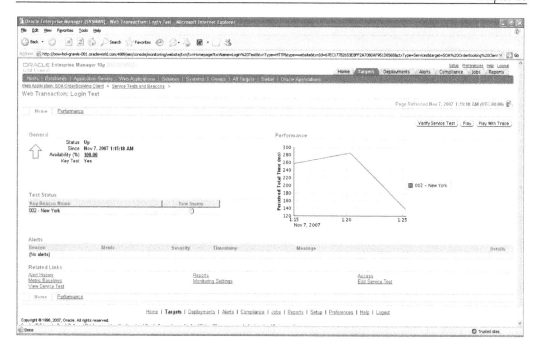

4. Observe the recorded transaction in the pop-up window.

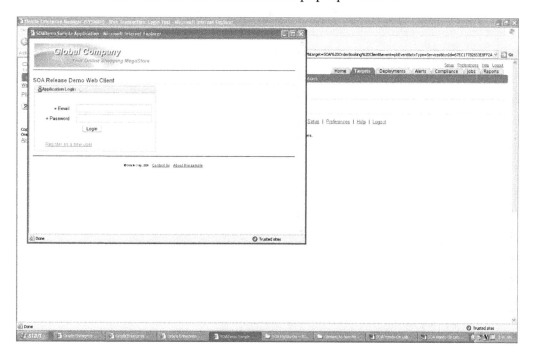

5. Observe the results of the test and the time breakdown for each component.

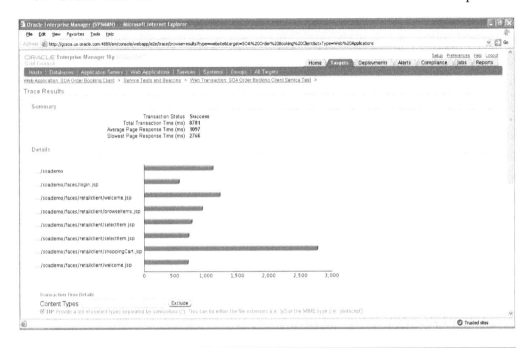

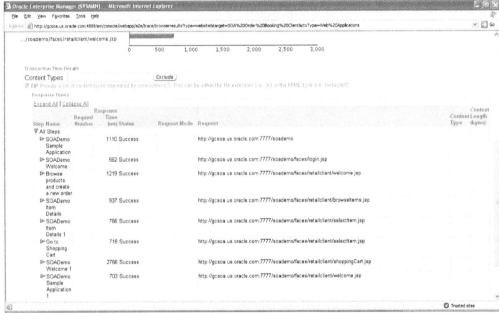

Summary

Recording and monitoring critical end-user paths is a proactive approach to increasing end-user satisfaction. In a global economy, enterprises need to ensure users can get the information they want, when they want it, from anywhere in the world. A management solution is incomplete without a synthetic monitoring strategy.

In this chapter, we discussed how to create web applications, record web transactions, and use specific metrics for performance and usage purposes. Further, we also discussed how to configure running these synthetic transactions from various agents or Beacons. Finally, we discussed how to view a web transaction to review and verify all the steps.

Synthetic service-test monitoring within Grid Control is complemented by passive real-user monitoring. Enterprise Manager's Real User Experience Insight (from the Moniforce acquisition) is a great tool in this area. More information on Real User Experience Insight can be found on the Oracle Technology Network.

11
Discovery of WebLogic and OSB targets

With the 10.2.0.5 (or 10gR5) release, Grid Control introduced new functionality for managing the **Oracle Service Bus (OSB)**, formerly known as the **AquaLogic Service Bus (ALSB)**. Grid Control had heterogeneous application server support even prior to 10.2.0.5. Specifically, Grid Control had monitoring functionality for the **WebLogic Server (WLS)**, going back to version 7.x. The introduction of OSB management complemented the WLS management functionality and helped strengthen Grid Control's middleware management offering to a considerable extent.

In the 10.2.0.5 release, Grid Control provided several features for OSB management such as discovering the OSB components, monitoring the OSB proxy and business services, monitoring the extended WebLogic and underlying infrastructure, deployment automation, configuration management, and service-level management.

This chapter talks about the discovery of the WebLogic Server and the OSB instance. Discovery of WebLogic and OSB is the first step before performing other management tasks. The following areas are covered in this chapter:

- Challenges
- Solution
- Step-by-step exercises:
  - ° Adding a WebLogic domain target
  - ° Navigating to the OSB target home page

Challenges

For any small, medium, or large enterprise, the challenge is to manage several disparate application, middleware, and database targets from a single console. The traditional hardware and software components such as servers, storage devices, operating systems, databases, middleware, and applications have been managed by system management solutions. With the rise of integration software such as BPEL and OSB, applications and infrastructure pose new problems. First, they need to be managed along with existing hardware and software. Second, as the WebLogic domains and OSB projects proliferate across the enterprise, the infrastructure team is faced with increasing problems to manage these projects. Thirdly, for the administrators who are new to OSB, supporting these environments in production poses unknown challenges. Finally, the IT managers want to avoid hiring new administrators with increasing OSB projects.

Solution

Grid Control provides a way to discover WebLogic and OSB components whether it is in development, test, stage, or production. For the infrastructure team, this is a convenient way to manage several installations from one console. The prerequisite is to have the Grid Control agent installed on the server hosting WebLogic admin server. Once the Grid Control agent is installed, the discovery process can be initiated from the console.

Step-by-step exercises

This set of step-by-step exercises will walkthrough discovering a WebLogic and OSB target.

Adding a WebLogic domain target

The first step in managing a WebLogic and OSB environment is to discover the WebLogic target—admin, clusters, and managed servers:

1. From the Grid Control home page, click on **Targets | Middleware**.
2. Click on the **Provisioning** sub-tab.

This is a view showing all of the monitored Middleware components in the enterprise. Grid Control can discover and manage several types of Application Servers such as Oracle Application Server, WebLogic, WebSphere, and JBoss. There are one or more target types and one or more targets for each piece of middleware that is discovered and managed. For each target, a summary of status with details, alerts, policy violations, CPU usage, and memory usage on the host are tabulated.

3. From the dropdown on the right, add an **Oracle WebLogic Server Domain** target. Click on **Go**, as shown in the following screenshot:

4. On the **Host** step, fill in the fields as shown in the next screenshot:

   ° Pick the **Administration Server Host** from the *flashlight*.

   ° **Version** as **10.x** (WebLogic Server version 7.x and above are supported).

   ° **Port** as **7021** (this is the default admin port).

   ° **Administration Server Username** as **weblogic**.

   ° **Password** as <Your WebLogic admin password>

   ° Check the **Save as Preferred Credentials** box.

   ° **Administration Server Home Directory** as **/u01/homes/osb_wls/wlserver_10.3/server/lib**.

   ° Leave the other fields blank.

   ° Click on **Next**.

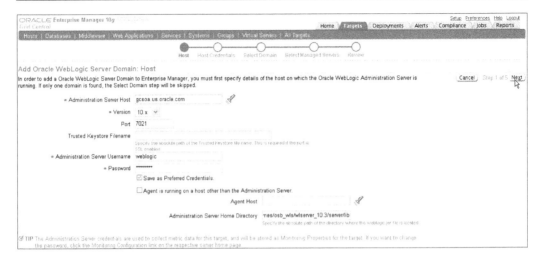

5. On the **Host Credentials** step:
   ° **Host Username** as **oracle**.
   ° **Password** as <*Your WebLogic admin password*>.
   ° Check the **Save as Preferred Credentials** box.
   ° Click on **Next**.

6. On the **Select Managed Servers** step:
   ° Check the domain that has been discovered with the Admin/ Managed Server and Oracle Service bus target.
   ° Click on **Next**, as shown in the next screenshot:

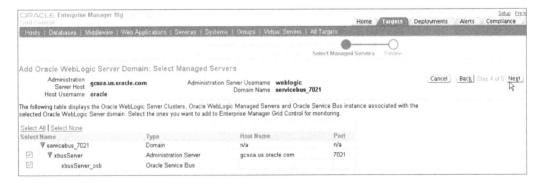

   ° On the **Review** step, click on **Finish**.
   ° On the **Middleware** page, observe the confirmation message. Look at the newly discovered WebLogic domain, Managed Server, and OSB target.

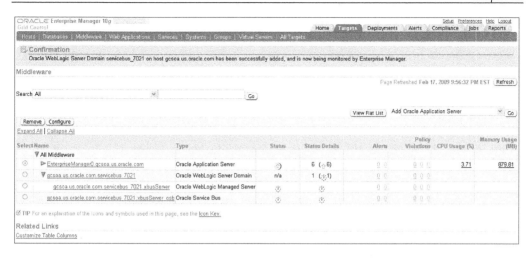

Navigating to the OSB target home page

Once the WebLogic and OSB components are discovered, it is useful to visit the OSB target home page and observe useful monitoring-related information.

- Click on the **Oracle Service Bus target name** hyperlink.

[
On the Oracle Service Bus target home page you will see the availability status of the OSB server, **Availability % (last 24 hours)**, **Oracle WebLogic Server Domain**, **Version**, and **Host**.
]

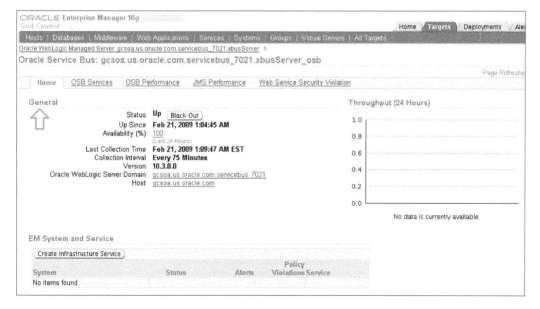

Summary

Discovery is the first step to managing a target in the enterprise. Discovering and managing multiple targets from a single console is a powerful way to ramp up on new projects, while maintaining a standardized management platform. This avoids hiring new administrators for new projects that increase the number of managed targets.

In this chapter, we looked at how to discover WebLogic Server and OSB targets. In particular, we discussed the mandatory discovery process to locate and identify the WebLogic and OSB components. There are several challenges associated with managing multiple components in the data center. Grid Control provides a single interface to discover and manage these disparate components. In the exercises, we walked through simple steps to discover WebLogic and OSB components. Finally, we viewed the key monitoring areas on the OSB target home page.

The WebLogic server discovery is mandatory, and OSB is discovered automatically as a result. These are mandatory steps to enable subsequent management tasks on WebLogic or OSB. The next few chapters will walkthrough hands-on exercises to set up and perform additional management tasks for the discovered targets.

12
OSB Deployment Automation

In most medium to large enterprises, integration developers have to deal with managing multiple initiatives spread over multiple departments. In the WebLogic and **Oracle Service Bus (OSB)** world, this translates to multiple WebLogic/OSB projects in multiple WebLogic domains. Typically, the integration developers are tasked with project development and testing while the WebLogic administrators are responsible for the deployment and operational support. This handoff is not entirely smooth due to different tools and processes in the development and operational organizations.

WebLogic administrators have to deal with multiple OSB projects. Typically, the OSB project deployment should follow the existing methodology in the enterprise. The operational team should centrally maintain the deployment artifacts, and this should be a different location than the one used by the development team. The deployment itself should be a well-defined procedure with a series of repeatable steps. Further, the set of best practices for the enterprise should be invoked at deployment time. This chapter talks about deploying multiple OSB projects to an OSB environment in a standardized manner. Specifically, this chapter talks about:

- Challenges
- Solution
- Step-by-step exercises:
    ° Viewing the Software Library
    ° Uploading projects to the Software Library
    ° Viewing the project deployment procedure
    ° Scheduling project deployment

Challenges

Deploying applications in production environments is a challenge. The SOA application developers build new projects, or new versions of existing projects, and throw them "over the wall" to the operations team. Administrators have to deploy multiple application files to multiple targets, in a fixed time window. This process is repeated when moving from test to stage to production. This consumes time and requires expertise on these applications. Controlling the WebLogic projects centrally is the first challenge, where administrators have to track the project versions to comply with change and release management guidelines. Next the deployment itself is a challenge, considering the administrator needs to deploy the projects with specific customizations and honor the scheduled maintenance window. All in all, the administrator has too many manual tasks to deal with, given the constraints of the operational environment.

Solution

With Grid Control, administrators can deploy multiple OSB projects to a domain deployment procedure framework. A five-step interview process lets the user pick the source projects, pick the target OSB server and domain, set the credentials, specify configurations and the customization file, and schedule a future deployment using the job system.

- Store OSB deployment artifacts in an enterprise Software Library
- Export OSB deployment artifacts from a live OSB server
- Track maturity of OSB deployment artifacts and usage
- Deploy OSB projects from test to stage to production
- Deploy in a future maintenance window

Step-by-step exercise

This set of step-by-step exercises will walkthrough managing the deployment of OSB projects.

Viewing the Software Library

The first step is to view the operational store or the Software Library in Grid Control. This is the starting point for administrators to look at the inventory, add items, or change existing items.

1. From the Grid Control home page, click on the **Deployments** tab.

2. Click the **Provisioning** sub-tab.

 The Software Library contains several objects such as operating system images, Oracle homes for database and application server, and deployment artifacts for BPEL, OSB, and so on. The Library is used to track the maturity of these components as they are used on various monitored targets.

3. Expand **Components** to reveal the component types.

Uploading projects to the Software Library

In this particular scenario, the administrator has been handed a copy of the OSB project, and needs to deploy it. Before deployment, the administrator needs to upload the projects to the Grid Control Software Library for tracking, operational version control, and to enable deployment:

1. Upload OSB Projects to Software Library

2. Select the radio button for **Oracle Components**.

3. Click on the **Create Component** button.

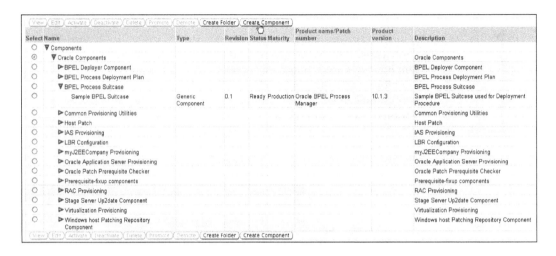

4. Enter the following values in the **Describe** step, as shown in the next screenshot:

  ° Select **Type** as **Generic Component**.

  ° Name as **OSB projects**.

  ° Leave the other fields blank.

  ° Click on **Next**.

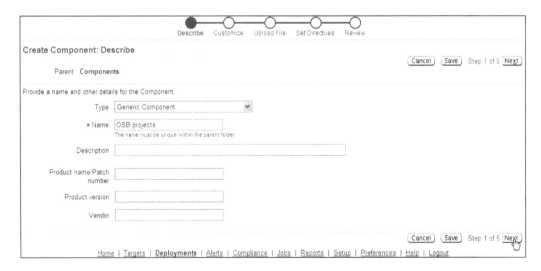

5. In the **Customize** step, leave the defaults and click on **Next**.

6. In the **Upload File** step:

  ° Select **Upload from Agent Machine**.

  ° Click on the **Select Target** button.

  ° Select the **Host Name** as **gcsoa.us.oracle.com**.

  ° Click on the **Select File** button.

  ° Select the location of the `sbconfig.jar` from a pre-existing project from an OSB server, which was zipped up and stored on the local machine; for instance: `/u01/homes/osb_wls/projects/sbconfig.jar`.

> Note that you can directly export projects from a live OSB server during the deployment process. This will be the most common usage of the deployment procedure. Here, for this workshop though, the export jar has already been created in advance. This export jar contains several projects extracted from another OSB server.

  ° Click on **Next**.

7. On the **Set Directives** step, click on **Next**.

8. On the **Review** step, note the details, and click on **Finish**.

9. Note the confirmation message, and the new **OSB Project** generic component that has been added.

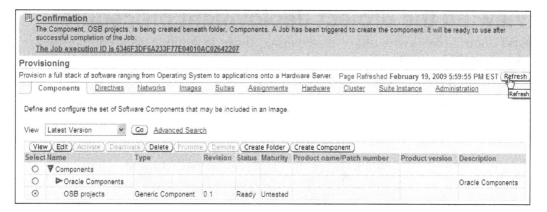

10. Activate the **OSB projects** for use:

    ° Select the radio button for **OSB Projects**.

    ° Click on **Activate**, as shown in the following screenshot:

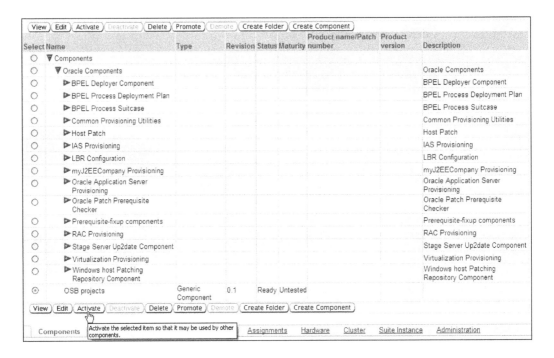

Viewing the project deployment procedure

Grid Control comes with out-of-the-box procedures to deploy Oracle components including OSB projects. These procedures simplify the administrator's life by automating manual steps, thereby saving time, and reducing human error.

1. View the **Oracle Service Bus Resource Provisioning** deployment procedure:

    ° From the Grid Control home page, click on the **Deployments** tab.

    ° Scroll down to locate the **Deployment Procedure Manager** section and click on the **Deployment Procedures** link.

A deployment procedure is a series of logical steps that automate key administrative tasks related to Oracle products. Most of these complex administrative tasks are listed in the "Enterprise Deployment Guide". Note the various deployment procedures available out of the box— database provisioning, RAC extend, application server provisioning, and many more. These deployment procedures can be customized as well.

- ° Search for "**service**" to locate the OSB deployment procedure.
- ° Click on the **Oracle Service Bus Resource Provisioning** link.

- ° Note the steps underlying the procedure and the orchestration of the steps.

Note that you can customize this procedure by adding steps at any point. You can do this by using the **Create Like** button.

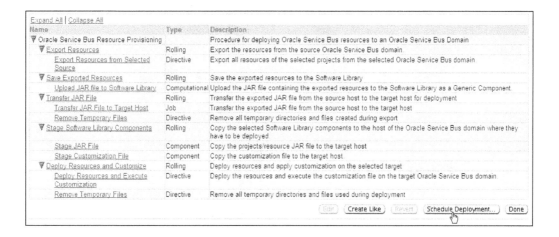

Scheduling project deployment

Now that we are familiar with the OSB project deployment procedure, the next step is to kick off the deployment. This can be done through a simple interview process:

1. Schedule the OSB project deployment.

2. Continuing from the previous step, click the **Schedule Deployment** button.

3. On the **Select Source** step, follow these steps:

    °   Select the **Oracle Software Library** radio button.

    °   Click the *Component* flashlight to locate the `jar` file from library.

    °   Locate the OSB projects that were uploaded previously.

    °   Click on **Select** to select source suitcase bundles.

 These bundles are stored in the Grid Control Software Library before actual deployment.

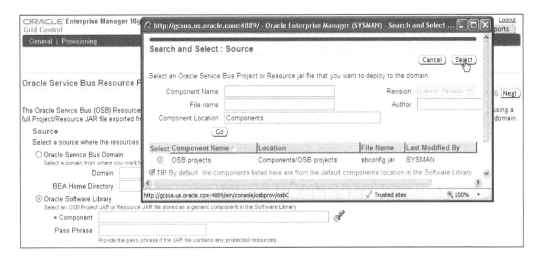

    °   Leave the pass phrase field blank.

    °   Click on **Next** to continue.

4. On the **Select Target** step:

    °   Select the relevant WebLogic domain from the flashlight.

    °   Specify the BEA home directory, for example: `/u01/homes/ osb_wls`.

○ Leave the **Advanced Options** section as it is.

○ Leave the **Customization File** option as it is.

 You can specify advanced options, as well as upload customization files, during deployment. The customization files could be uploaded to the Software Library and reused for deployments to development, stage, test, and production.

○ Click on **Next** to proceed, as shown in the following screenshot:

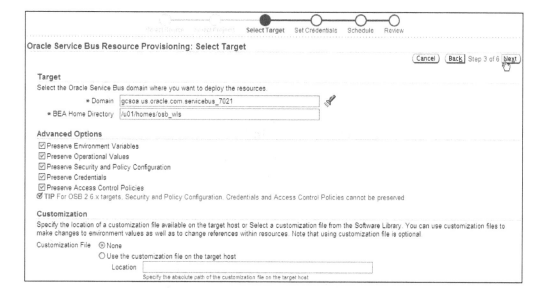

5. In the **Set Credentials** step:

○ Provide the credentials for OSB Domain. If you checked the **Store Preferred Credentials** box during target discovery, then the **Username** and **Password** fields are auto-populated for you.

○ Provide the credentials for the host. If you checked the **Store Preferred Credentials** box during target discovery, then the **Username** and **Password** fields are again auto-populated for you.

    °   Click on **Next** to proceed, as shown in the following screenshot:

6.   In the **Schedule** step, follow these steps:

    °   Select **One Time (Immediately)**.

    °   Leave **Grace Period** as **Indefinite**.

    °   Leave the default name **OSB Resource Provisioning_1235085922548** for the **Instance Name** field, or specify a new name

    °   Click on **Next** to proceed, as shown in the following screenshot:

Deployment can be scheduled immediately or for a future time, typically during a customer maintenance window. The Grid Control job system takes care of the job scheduling and management.

7. In the **Review** step:

  ° Review all the information before submitting a deployment job.

  ° Click on **Finish** when you're ready.

8. View the status of the scheduled deployment:

  ° Continuing from the previous step, click on the deployment job from the confirmation screen.

  ° The job status page shows the details of the scheduled job, including elapsed time and error messages if any.

  ° Use the **Refresh** button on the top right to see the progress.

      °   Wait for the job to finish successfully.

      °   Note the **Status** and **Completed Date** values.

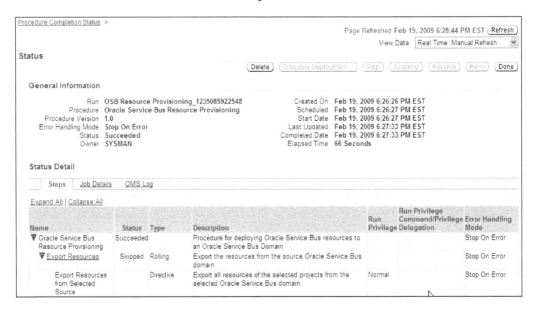

9.   View the deployed projects in Grid Control:

      °   Navigate to the OSB target home page.

      °   Click on the **OSB Services** tab.

      °   Click the **Refresh** button on the top right.

      °   Note the newly deployed projects in the list.

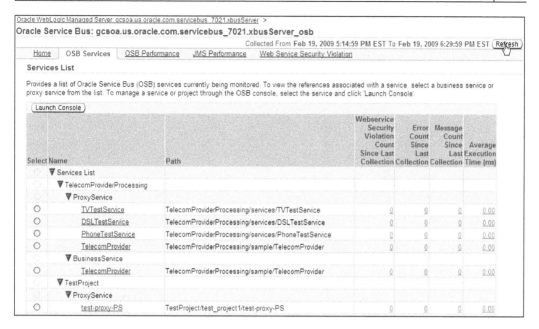

Summary

Deployment is a critical task for WebLogic administrators. With Grid Control Software Library and deployment procedure capabilities, administrators can manage WebLogic and OSB projects, and schedule and automate deployment.

In this chapter, we covered the various administrative challenges dealing with application code deployments such as OSB project deployments. Grid Control automates the deployment process for the administrator, thereby saving time and reducing human errors. First we took a look at the Grid Control Software Library, then we uploaded the new OSB projects to this library, and then we kicked off the actual deployment procedure. Finally, we looked at the execution of the deployment procedure job, and validated the completion and successful deployment via the OSB console.

The next few chapters will walkthrough managing other areas in OSB such as monitoring services, managing configurations, and service levels.

13
OSB Proxy and Business Service Monitoring

Oracle Service Bus is one of the premier **Enterprise Service Bus (ESB)** systems available in the marketplace. It follows the typical ESB paradigm of validate, enrich, and transform (VET). Often, OSB acts as the provider to one or more consumers for business critical services.

Monitoring provides visibility and the means to measure availability and performance, and hence evaluate service-level agreements between providers and consumers. This chapter talks about monitoring OSB proxy and business services. Specifically, this chapter talks about:

- Challenges
- Solution
- Step-by-step exercises:
    ° Creating an OSB infrastructure service
    ° Navigating to the OSB proxy service home page
    ° Creating the OSB proxy aggregate service
    ° Creating a SOAP test to monitor a OSB proxy service endpoint
    ° Creating a SOAP test to monitor a OSB business service endpoint
    ° Testing the SOAP tests

Challenges

For any small, medium, or large enterprise, it's a challenge to monitor several disparate application, middleware, and database targets from a single console. The traditional hardware and software components such as servers, storage devices, operating systems, databases, middleware, and applications have been monitored by system management solutions. With the rise of integration software such as BPEL and OSB, applications and infrastructure pose new problems. First, they need to be monitored along with existing hardware and software. Second, as the WebLogic domains and OSB projects proliferate across the enterprise, the infrastructure team is faced with increasing problems to manage these projects. Thirdly, for the administrators who are new to OSB, supporting these environments in production poses unknown challenges. Finally, the IT managers want to avoid hiring new administrators with increasing OSB projects.

Solution

Grid Control provides monitoring capabilities for WebLogic and OSB components whether it is in development, test, stage, or production. For the infrastructure team, this is a convenient way to monitor several installations from one console. Once the Grid Control agent is installed on the server hosting WebLogic Admin Server, the discovery process can be initiated from the console. Post discovery, the infrastructure components and OSB services can be monitored from Grid Control.

Step-by-step exercises

This set of step-by-step exercises will walkthrough monitoring proxy and business services.

Creating an OSB Infrastructure Service

The OSB infrastructure service provides a useful grouping to monitor relevant OSB and WebLogic components as a whole. Grid Control takes care of identifying the relationships among the infrastructure components and putting them in one bucket.

1. From the Grid Control home page, click on **Targets | Middleware**.
2. Expand the WebLogic Server Domain target of your choice and click on the OSB target.
3. From the OSB target home page, click on the **Create Infrastructure Service** button.

4. On the **Create Service** page, enter a **Service Name** such as **osb_infra** and click on **OK**, as shown in the following screenshot:

5. You should get a **confirmation** message. Click on **OK**.

The infrastructure service encapsulates the key underlying logical components of the OSB instance. For the OSB instance and services to work smoothly, the underlying infrastructure must work smoothly as well. Observe the newly created system and service, status of system and service, alerts, and policy violations.

Navigating to the OSB proxy service home page

Proxy services perform the heavy lifting for the OSB. They are created to validate, enrich, and transform messages coming into the service bus. It is extremely important for the administrator to have visibility and understanding of the OSB proxy services.

1. From the OSB target home page, click on the **OSB Services** tab.

All the OSB services deployed on the server are automatically discovered and displayed here. Summary throughput process instance information is also displayed in the table. These metric values are collected at a frequency controlled by the "Collection Interval" directly from the OSB server and stored in the Grid Control metric repository. It is possible to drill down on any metric to view trends for different functions such as minimum, maximum, or average values over a specific time range.

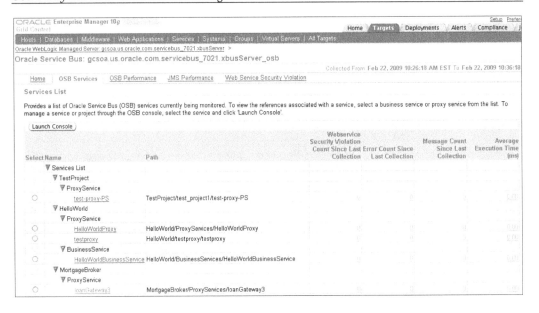

2. Click on any of the deployed proxy services within a project, for example, **loanGateway3** proxy service under the **MortgageBroker** project.

This is the individual OSB proxy service page. Note the proxy specific instance throughput graph. At the bottom, note that all the references for the proxy are discovered along with the business services, endpoints, protocols, load-balancing algorithms, weight, and so on.

Creating the OSB proxy aggregate service

An aggregate service is a useful structural entity in Grid Control to provide a relationship and hierarchy among OSB proxy, business, and infrastructure services. When troubleshooting a problem, it is useful not only to know the state of a proxy service, but also the state of the supporting infrastructure.

1. From the OSB proxy page, under **EM Services** click on the **Create Service** button.

2. Notice the confirmation message, and the aggregate service that has been added.

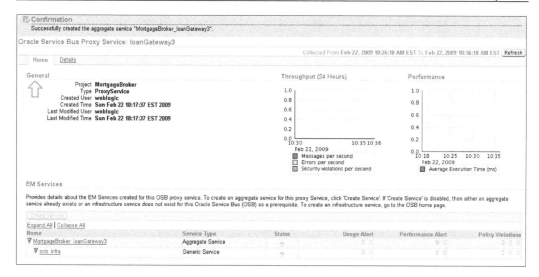

Note that the aggregate service that was created is listed under the **Services** section. The previously created infrastructure service has automatically been associated with the aggregate service. In the **Services** section, starting from the left, you see the service name, type of service, status, and other alerts. The top-level service is the aggregate service. The next service is the infrastructure service — a subservice of the aggregate.

Creating a SOAP test to monitor an OSB proxy service endpoint

Monitoring proxy services from a client or an end-user perspective is important for the operations team. This helps the team to get alerted potentially before clients or end users report the error.

A **SOAP (Simple Object Access Protocol)** test is a way to check the availability and performance of a Web service with a SOAP interface. This remote synthetic check invokes an operation within the Web service as defined in the **WSDL (Web Service Description Language)** and measure the HTTP response code and latency.

1. Scroll down to the **References** section, and select **loanGateway3** from the radio button list.

2. Click on the **Add SOAP Test** button to create a SOAP test for that service.

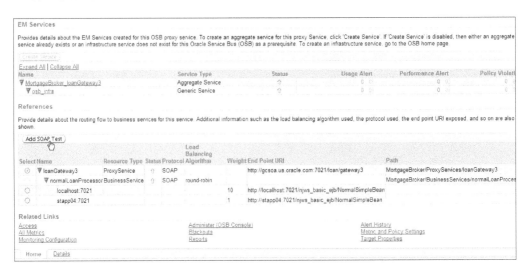

3. For the **Collection Frequency** field, enter **3 minutes**.

4. Under **Input Parameters**, click on **XML Source**.

5. Enter a proxy service payload. This is the XML input that is needed for the proxy service to perform its business.

A proxy service payload can be generated through a simple test of the proxy through the OSB console. Once the inputs are entered into the test page, the console generates an XML payload that can be used as input for the SOAP test.

6. Leave the **Basic Authentication Credentials** section empty.

7. Click on **Continue**, as shown in the following screenshot:

8. To add a Beacon, click on the **Add** button.

9. From the pop-up window, check one or more Beacons from the available Beacons and click on **Select**, as shown in the following screenshot:

10. Click on **OK** to save the SOAP test and Beacon settings.

11. On the OSB proxy home page, note the availability generic service that was automatically created.

 The availability service for the OSB proxy is formed when the first SOAP test is created. Note the status of each test, and how it is rolled up (configurable) to determine process availability.

12. Expand the **loanGateway3_availability** and verify whether the SOAP test that was just created in the prior steps has been added.

Note that the status of the SOAP test will take some time to show up, based on the frequency set for the test.

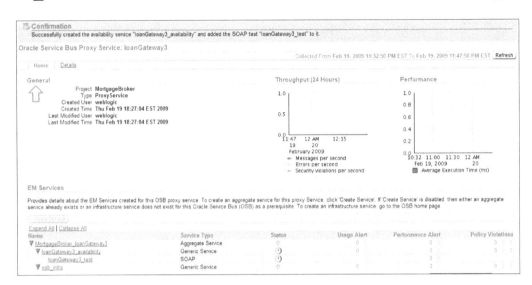

Creating a SOAP test to monitor an OSB business service endpoint

Business services provide the endpoint facade to the proxy services. It is important to monitor them with SOAP tests similar to the proxy service monitoring.

1. Create a business service SOAP test to monitor business service endpoint.

2. Go to the **loanGateway3** proxy page.

3. Scroll down and select one of the business service endpoints, for example the **localhost:7021** radio button under the **normalLoanProcessor** business service.

4. Click on **Add SOAP Test** to create a SOAP test for the business service.

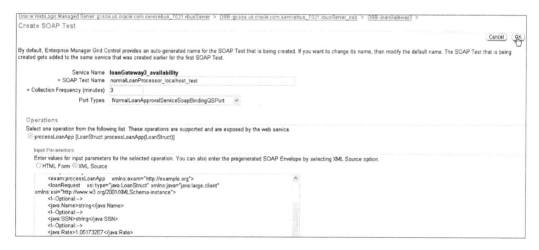

5. Change the collection frequency to a desired number in minutes, for instance, **3**.

6. Leave the default port that has been selected.

7. Under **Input Parameters**, click on **XML Source**.

8. Enter the business service payload saved earlier.

9. Leave the **Basic Authentication Credentials** section empty.

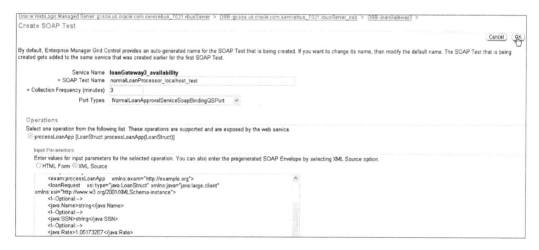

10. Click on **OK** to complete the creation of the service test.

11. Observe the confirmation message.

12. Expand the availability service to view the SOAP test for the business service endpoint.

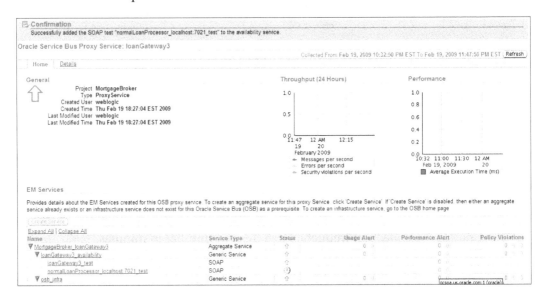

Testing the SOAP tests

Once the SOAP tests have been created, Grid Control provides the capability to run any of the SOAP tests on demand to test the availability and performance of the underlying service.

1. Click on one of the SOAP tests that you've created.

 The test page shows the test availability, Beacons that run this test, and alerts associated with this test. The graph shows the test response times from the beacon. Note that the test metrics will take some time to show up on the test home page. One or more Beacons could be used to test the service, potentially from multiple geographic locations that emulate the user base.

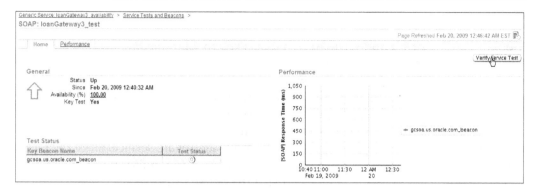

2. Click on the **Verify Service Test** button.

3. Click on the **Perform Test** to run the test instantaneously and view the results, as shown in the following screenshot:

Summary

Monitoring OSB proxy and business services is key to guaranteeing healthy key business processes in the enterprise, and preserving the provider-to-consumer relationship. In this chapter, we looked at how to monitor OSB proxy and business services using agent-based monitoring and synthetic tests. In order to monitor the OSB services, the appropriate Grid Control service mappings had to be created. We created the OSB infrastructure service, visited the proxy service home page to view the discovered services, and created the OSB proxy aggregate service. Once the Grid Control services had been set up, we created SOAP tests to monitor the proxy and business service endpoints. Finally, we tested the SOAP tests that we created.

The next few chapters will walkthrough hands-on exercises to perform additional management tasks on the Oracle Service Bus.

14
WebLogic and OSB Configuration Management

Managing the configurations of middleware environments is a difficult proposition for medium and large enterprises. "Knowing what you have" enables IT managers to make decisions about future investments and retiring old assets, standardize existing assets, manage change across the enterprise, and troubleshoot performance problems related to configurations.

Most configuration management solutions today are compliant with the best practices laid out by the **IT Information Library (ITIL)** framework. All the assets are stored in a central repository called the **Configuration Management Database (CMDB)**. Configuration parameters such as instance parameters for a database, or start up parameters for a WebLogic application server, or port numbers for an HTTP server are stored in the CMDB. Any changes to these parameters are also tracked. It then becomes easy to audit the changes for a specific asset, compare assets to each other (for example, Managed Server 1 and Managed Server 2), compare different versions of the same asset, save a reference configuration to the CMDB, and use that to standardize across the enterprise. This chapter talks about managing configurations for a WebLogic and OSB environment. Specifically, this chapter talks about:

- Challenges
- Solution
- Step-by-step exercises:
    - Viewing a WebLogic managed server configuration
    - Saving a managed server configuration snapshot
    - Viewing and saving an OSB configuration
    - Comparing the current OSB configuration with a saved baseline
    - Comparing the current managed server configuration with a saved baseline

Challenges

It is difficult to track the configurations of all IT systems. Often, IT departments resort to Excel spreadsheets to store critical middleware configuration information. This makes an IT department slow in making changes, measuring impact, identifying performance problems due to incorrect configuration, and increases costs of managing a data center. With a WebLogic and OSB environment, it is difficult to maintain configurations for multiple domains, and underlying configurations. For a medium-to-large WebLogic installation, it is important to baseline a working configuration and compare it with non-working ones for department or enterprise-wide customization. For OSB, there is the additional challenge of maintaining the proxy and business service configurations over different project versions. In the absence of control over configurations, it is difficult to assess the production impact for new project versions, as well as troubleshoot production problems that might be associated with configuration changes.

Solution

With Grid Control, key configuration metrics for WebLogic and OSB server processes are collected and stored in the Enterprise Manager repository. Administrators can view the historic configuration changes across the WebLogic and OSB environment. They can also baseline a working configuration by saving it in the repository. A WebLogic Admin, Managed Server, and OSB server configuration parameters can be compared with other servers. Finally, OSB project versions can also be compared to observe the changes and assess impact across successive deployments.

Step-by-step exercises

This set of step-by-step exercises will walkthrough managing configurations for the WebLogic and OSB server targets.

Viewing a WebLogic managed server configuration

During a reactive troubleshooting exercise (typically associated with a monitoring alert), one of the first questions that an administrator asks is "what changed?" Before even viewing the changes, it is useful to look at the current configuration of the system to determine if there are any obvious wrong settings:

1. Navigate to the **Targets | Middleware** tab.
2. Click on the **Oracle WebLogic Managed Server** link.

3. This takes you to the Managed Server home page.

4. Click on the **Administration** tab.

5. Note the links related to Configuration Management for the target.

 The Grid Control Configuration Management framework picks up key configuration parameters for WebLogic components including the Managed Server and Admin Server on a daily basis. These parameters are stored in the Grid Control repository. Key configuration tasks can be accessed from here.

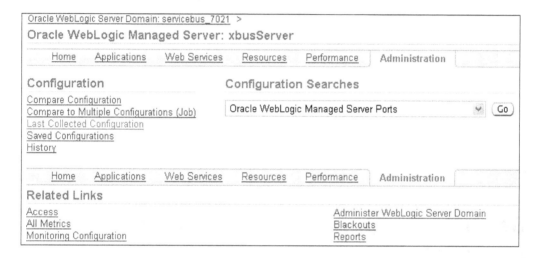

6. Notice that you can launch **Configuration Searches** from here for data sources, applications, J2EE modules, ports, and so on.

7. View the last collected configuration for the managed server:

   ° Click on **Last Collected Configuration** to view configuration parameters.

   ° View the configuration settings on the **Last Collected Configuration** page.

   ° The **General** tab shows generic information about the server including ports, resource usage, tuning parameters, JVM info, and cluster parameters.

   ° The **Applications** tab lists the deployed applications, along with the path. It also shows modules, type, URL mapping, and session timeout information.

   ° **JDBC Resources** shows a list of connection pools and data sources.

- ° **JMS Resources** specifies queues, max/min byte size if configured, JNDI name, and so on.

- ° **Virtual Hosts** shows the list of hosts if configured.

- ° **Miscellaneous** shows startup/shutdown classes, Jolt connection pools, and work manager information.

- ° **Configuration Files** shows the list of key configuration files for the managed server.

- ° Drill down into a configuration file to view the contents.

Saving a managed server configuration snapshot

Standardizing a managed server configuration is important to ensure predictable behavior across multiple installations. The first step toward standardization is saving an existing, trustworthy configuration in the Grid Control repository, so that it can be used as a standard for comparing with other configurations:

1. Drill down into a configuration file to view the contents

2. Click on the **Save** button on the top right.

3. Select the option to **Save to Enterprise Manager Repository**.

4. Enter a description such as **ManagedServerGoldConfig**, as shown in the following screenshot:

5. Click on **OK** to save the current configuration to the EM repository.

6. Note the confirmation message and the saved configuration with timestamp, name, description, saved date, and owner.

Viewing and saving an OSB configuration

Similar to the WebLogic Managed Server target, we can also view the latest configuration for the OSB target, and save a known, trustworthy configuration to the Grid Control repository:

1. Navigate to the **Configuration Management** section for an OSB target:

    ° Navigate to the OSB target home page.

    ° At the bottom, under **Configuration**, click on the **View Configuration** tab.

2. View the last collected configuration for the OSB target:

    ° The current configuration of the OSB server is displayed.

    ° Notice the JMS queue information (specific queues to the OSB).

    ° OSB frontend configuration and global operation settings capture key parameters that are set on the OSB console.

   ◦ Proxy and Business service configurations are displayed for each deployed service.

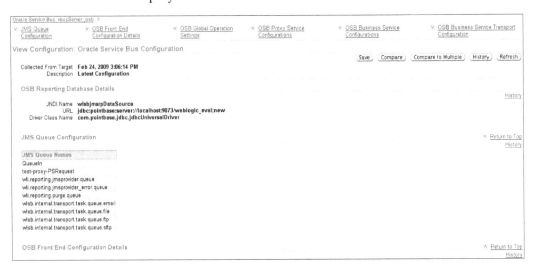

3. Save a configuration snapshot to the repository:

  ◦ Click on the **Save** button to save the current configuration.

  ◦ Select the option to **Save to EM Repository**.

  ◦ Provide a description such as **OSBGoldConfig**.

  ◦ Click on **OK** to save the current configuration to the EM repository.

  ◦ Note the confirmation message and the saved configuration with target name, target type, and timestamp.

Comparing the current OSB configuration with a saved baseline

Once the OSB configuration snapshot has been saved in Grid Control, this can be used as a standard for comparing with other OSB targets. Often, it is useful to compare the static trustworthy snapshot with the latest configuration, in order to see the drift from the known, trustworthy state.

To view configuration changes, you must make some changes on the OSB console before attempting this section. For example, log in to the OSB console, and change "Global Settings" and some business and proxy service configuration. Then you can attempt this section to view the changes picked up in Grid Control.

1. Update the latest configuration:
   - ° Navigate to the OSB target home page.
   - ° Click on the **View Configuration** link at the bottom.
   - ° Click on the **Refresh** button to get the latest configurations updated.
   - ° Wait for a minute. Grid Control agents interact with the OSB server to get the latest information and display it on the page.

2. Initiate configuration comparison:
   - ° Click on the **Compare** button to start a comparison between the current configuration of the OSB target and a saved ("**OSBGold Config**") configuration.
   - ° Click on the **Saved Configuration** link.
   - ° Select the **OSBGoldConfig** for comparison.

3. Click on **Compare** to generate the comparison results.

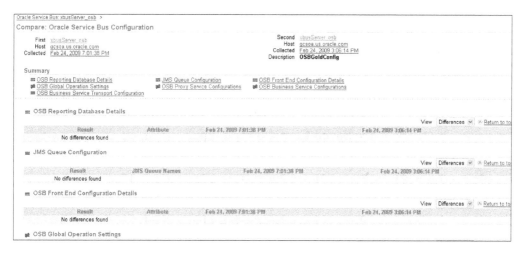

4. View the OSB target comparison results with a saved baseline:

- ° The comparison results between the OSB targets are presented in all the categories. The **Summary** tab lists the status of the categories.

- ° Notice the differences marked with a red *inequality* sign for the various parameters.

Comparing the current managed server configuration with a saved baseline

Just as we compared an OSB server configuration with a saved snapshot, we can also compare the WebLogic managed server target with the saved snapshot. This will enable us to identify the configuration differences at the WebLogic level.

 To view configuration changes, you must make some changes on the WebLogic admin console before attempting this section. For example, login to the Admin console, and change some settings for the Managed Server in question. Then you can attempt this section to view the changes picked up in Grid Control.

1. Update the latest configuration:

- ° Navigate to the Managed Server target home page.

- ° Click on the **Administration** tab.

- ° Click on the **Last Collected Configuration** button to get the latest configurations updated.

- ° Click on **Refresh** to update the latest configuration.

- ° Wait for a minute.

2. Initiate configuration comparison:

- ° Click on the **Compare** button to start a comparison between the current configuration of the Managed Server target and a saved (**ManagedServerGoldConfig**) configuration.

- ° Click on the **Saved Configuration** link.

- ° Select **ManagedServerGoldConfig** for comparison.

3. View the differences between the current and the saved configurations:

    °   Click on **Configuration Files**.

    °   Select **config.xml**.

    °   Click on **Compare File Contents**.

    °   Observe the differences marked in red.

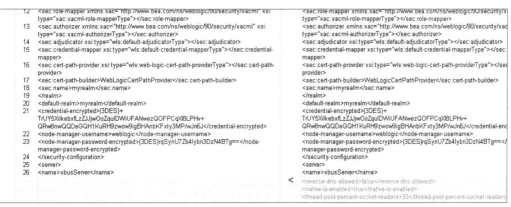

Summary

Configuration management is critical for administrators to control change within the environment and troubleshoot problems associated with changing configurations. With Grid Control's configuration management capabilities, administrators can manage change and reduce time to troubleshoot problems.

In this chapter, we discussed the challenges related to configurations in the enterprise. We discussed how to view the latest configuration for WebLogic managed server and OSB targets. Then we saved a snapshot of a known, trustworthy configuration in the Grid Control repository, so we could use that as a baseline for comparison. Then we compared the saved baseline with the latest configuration and viewed the drift. We discussed how the Grid Control configuration features could be leveraged for the WebLogic managed server and the OSB target.

Configuration management has been extended with Enterprise Manager's acquisition of two new products, namely **Configuration Change Console (CCC)** and **Application Change Console (ACC)**. With these two products, administrators can view changes actively as they happen, as well as roll back and roll forward to a desired configuration.

Index

Z

Thank you for buying

BPEL PM and OSB operational management with Oracle Enterprise Manager 10*g* Grid Control

About Packt Publishing

Packt, pronounced 'packed', published its first book "Mastering phpMyAdmin for Effective MySQL Management" in April 2004 and subsequently continued to specialize in publishing highly focused books on specific technologies and solutions.

Our books and publications share the experiences of your fellow IT professionals in adapting and customizing today's systems, applications, and frameworks. Our solution based books give you the knowledge and power to customize the software and technologies you're using to get the job done. Packt books are more specific and less general than the IT books you have seen in the past. Our unique business model allows us to bring you more focused information, giving you more of what you need to know, and less of what you don't.

Packt is a modern, yet unique publishing company, which focuses on producing quality, cutting-edge books for communities of developers, administrators, and newbies alike. For more information, please visit our website: www.packtpub.com.

About Packt Enterprise

In 2010, Packt launched two new brands, Packt Enterprise and Packt Open Source, in order to continue its focus on specialization. This book is part of the Packt Enterprise brand, home to books published on enterprise software – software created by major vendors, including (but not limited to) IBM, Microsoft and Oracle, often for use in other corporations. Its titles will offer information relevant to a range of users of this software, including administrators, developers, architects, and end users.

Writing for Packt

We welcome all inquiries from people who are interested in authoring. Book proposals should be sent to author@packtpub.com. If your book idea is still at an early stage and you would like to discuss it first before writing a formal book proposal, contact us; one of our commissioning editors will get in touch with you.

We're not just looking for published authors; if you have strong technical skills but no writing experience, our experienced editors can help you develop a writing career, or simply get some additional reward for your expertise.

Oracle SOA Suite 11g R1 Developer's Guide

ISBN: 978-1-849680-18-9   Paperback: 720 pages

Develop Service-Oriented Architecture Solutions with the Oracle SOA Suite

1. A hands-on, best-practice guide to using and applying the Oracle SOA Suite in the delivery of real-world SOA applications

2. Detailed coverage of the Oracle Service Bus, BPEL PM, Rules, Human Workflow, Event Delivery Network, and Business Activity Monitoring

3. Master the best way to use and combine each of these different components in the implementation of a SOA solution

SOA Patterns with BizTalk Server 2009

ISBN: 978-1-847195-00-5   Paperback: 400 pages

Implement SOA strategies for BizTalk Server solutions

1. Discusses core principles of SOA and shows them applied to BizTalk solutions

2. The most thorough examination of BizTalk and WCF integration in any available book

3. Leading insight into the new WCF SQL Server Adapter, UDDI Services version 3, and ESB Guidance 2.0

Please check **www.PacktPub.com** for information on our titles

Middleware Management with Oracle Enterprise Manager Grid Control 10g R5

ISBN: 978-1-847198-34-1   Paperback: 350 pages

Monitor, diagnose, and maximize the system performance of Oracle Fusion Middleware solutions

1. Manage your Oracle Fusion Middleware and non-Oracle middleware applications effectively and efficiently using Oracle Enterprise Manager Grid Conrol

2. Implement proactive monitoring to maximize application performance

3. A Hands-on tutorial detailing Oracle Enterprise Manager Grid Control's management of Middleware

SOA Cookbook

ISBN: 978-1-847195-48-7   Paperback: 268 pages

Master SOA process architecture, modeling, and simulation in BPEL, TIBCO's BusinessWorks, and BEA's Weblogic Integration

1. Lessons include how to model orchestration, how to build dynamic processes, how to manage state in a long-running process, and numerous others

2. BPEL tools discussed include BPEL simulator, BPEL compiler, and BPEL complexity analyzer

3. Examples in BPEL, TIBCO's BusinessWorks, BEA's Weblogic Integration

Please check **www.PacktPub.com** for information on our titles